CREATIVE APPROACHES TO CLASSROOM TEACHING

CREATIVE APPROACHES TO CLASSROOM TEACHING

Dr. Joseph C. Mukalel
M.A., M.Ed., M.A.(U.K.), Ph.D.
School of Gandhian Thought
and Development Studies,
Mahatma Gandhi University,
Kottayam (Kerala)

DISCOVERY PUBLISHING HOUSE
NEW DELHI

Reprinted - 2019

First Published - 1998

ISBN: 978-81-7141-401-7

Creative Approaches to Classroom Teaching

Published by:

DISCOVERY PUBLISHING HOUSE PVT. LTD.

4383/4B, Ansari Road, Darya Ganj
New Delhi-110 002 (India)
Phone: +91-11-23279245, 23253475; 43596065
E-mail: discoverybooksindia@gmail.com
discoverypublishinghouse@gmail.com
web: www.discoverypublishinggroup.com

Printed at:
Infinity Imaging Systems
Delhi

CONTENTS

INTRODUCTION

The most dangerous thing about any system is that it tends to get stratified and routinised with the result that it, in course of time, begins to degenerate. This is inevitable if the system does not find a level of development. Teaching is inherently dynamic but like any other system it faces the danger of routinisation and degeneration. Teaching is a professional but unlike other professions teaching directly deals with the formation of human persons. The classroom where this process of formation takes place is by any criterion most sacred. Men of all other professions, as we know, receive formation in the classroom and the uniqueness of teaching can be traced back to this fundamental role.

For this reason we are inviting social and moral catastrophe the moment we try to commercialise our practice in the classroom. The dangers are several. The teacher remains always relatively low-paid and this generates in him a sense of inferiority regarding his social status and things related to it. This feeling significantly affects his classroom practice and brings down his morale. There is a greater sense of security attached to this profession and the teacher tends easily to fall prey to lethargy. The teacher by and large remains more educated than those belonging to other professions. This arouses in him a feeling that no more reading, study or preparation is required of him, and that he knows more than what is required in the classroom. This sense of adequacy is a great danger to his professional growth. The awareness and the feeling that there at his command only a tip of the ice-berg of knowledge for his use is very necessary for the professional growth of the teacher.

A large variety of factors keep the teacher's creative efforts low. Because of this, as stated above, he has the constant tendency to remain where he is and become a victim of the dissipation of energy subject to which any system degenerates. The principal solution to this dangerous tendency would be to keep the teacher's creative efforts at a much higher plan. It is true that the teacher lacks the necessary motivation for different reasons. But he cannot leave things simply at that level. He is a professional and this fact of being a professional should function as the highest motivating factor for his creative efforts. The skilled training of an occupation, the specialised education of a profession and the call and commitment of a vocation are all coherently combined together in teaching. This commitment and call of a vocation elevate teaching to a plain much higher than what is ordinarily recognised.

It is, therefore, necessary to elevate teaching in the classroom to a higher level of creativity. The present work attempts to highlight creative classroom practices of all sorts conceived of as parallel to the traditional ways. The chapter on the lecture method provides ways and means to render lecture a more meaningful, varied and creative activity. Lecture as an essential and unavoidable method of teaching can be raised from the plain of mere telling and explanation. The chapter recommends ways of introducing into the lecture a whole range of interactional components most useful to students.

The chapter on the group method of teaching investigates into the possibilities and potentials of group dynamism and its role in teaching - learning situations. Group method of teaching is found to be the most interaction - oriented and dynamic of all teaching methods. This is the place where we leave the responsibility of learning to the students themselves. Learning is expected to take place through most productive interaction and discussion among the members of the particular group. It is ordinarily not possible to convert all learning into exclusive group method type. But enlightened teachers can make the most creative use of this method.

Teaching through tutorials and seminars is recognised to be very productive especially at higher levels of education. Rudiments of these can be introduced even at the school level. In tutorials and seminars the students are given assignments beforehand to have this own preparation. This can be done on any elementary topics. This method generates, again, student involvement of a much higher type. This method enables them to handle more comprehensive concept and develop materials on this own.

The chapter on the workshop method of teaching presents a unique treatment of classroom teaching techniques. Workshops are conceived of as a locale for the production of materials.

Workshops will function where most concrete learning topics need to be handled. Students learn how to produce academic, learning materials. At the college classes especially this method will be found to be most productive when students sit down in groups and produce academic materials of their own for study purposes. The project method of teaching is well known for its inherent dynamism and pragmatic utility. Learning becomes centred on a project. The project, whatever be its nature, generates a whole range of activities and experiences. It becomes the fulcrum of learning as envisaged by the pragmatic educationist. The teacher guides the student to develop and organise materials so as to create a well-defined project.

The classroom is meant not only for the provision of information on classified subjects but also for the development of all sorts of communicative abilities. The teaching of languages aims primarily at the development of such communicative potentials. The chapter on communicative strategies deal with a whole range of problems related to the development of this communicative potential of the student. The chapter on new approaches to classroom interaction makes an attempt to view classroom interaction from a strictly methodological view point. The teacher's insight into classroom interaction will be of immense help to transform teaching into a highly creative activity. The chapter on the global techniques which are common to all levels and areas of teaching. New insights are provided to these techniques by means of which teaching at all levels can be made creative and interesting. Chapter 9 deals with the design and the use of low-cost aids. The teacher needs to be equipped with the art of preparing and using his own low-cost teaching aids that would make his work in the classroom effective. The chapter on the academic skill of reference provides important insights into the way training into the reference of materials may be obtained, a skill most fundamental to an individual's academic life. The teacher is open to countless ways of making teaching a creative and productive effort.

1

LECTURE METHOD

ASPECTS AND TECHNIQUES

1. Teaching, a Science

The fundamental question regarding teaching in the classroom has always been whether teaching is *an art* or *a Science*. The pendulum has always lead us to the extremes and schools in education, and educational theories have focussed on one aspect or other. The *mechanical aspects* of classroom practices on the one hand and the *creative dimensions* of the classroom on the other have created polarities in theory and practice. The contributions of behavioural psychology and in particular of behaviourism as well as those of cognitive-field psychologies towards these dichotomens polarities have been significant, and these show how crucial the two perspectives are in our understanding of the theory and practices of teaching.

A systemic understanding of teaching as envisaged in the present work focuses on teaching as a Science. Teaching is a Science. As a system of classroom practices, teaching also has a genuinely creative and artistic dimension which the teacher keeps in mind while dealing with students in the classroom. The holistic approach that is recommended for creative teaching should in practice be brought down to earth to a *systems analysis* that gives the teacher confidence in dealing with the components that constitute the building-blocks of the system of teaching. This helps the teacher avoid much groping in the dark and resort to most effective classroom techniques for successful teaching.

2. A Systemic Approach To Teaching

The most effective perspective that we can have of teaching practices consists of what can be called a systems approach. Systems Analysis has become the catchword of the day. All entities in this universe are viewed in this case as a system of one kind or other with a definite purpose for this survival as systems. Systems approach leads to considerably deep interaction among and unification of disciplines, organizations and individuals. Several aspects of systems approach are most relevant to education in general and teaching in particular. It makes clear that no problem in any area is isolated in its origin and thus cannot be solved in its own isolation. Just as all entities in this universe are interrelated with respect to this systemic liaison, all problems that require solution need to be viewed from associated and larger problems to arrive at a feasible solution.

Systemic approach has to view all objects of its study from three complex notions: (a) sub-systems, (b) systems, and (c) Super systems. In other words all systems communicate and interact with this sub-systems on the one hand and super systems on the other. This communication is the very essence of the survival of any entity as a system. As we look around we have ample proofs for this phenomenon. Smaller things, people and nations constantly find this movements and affairs constrained by bigger things, people and nations. It is possible to realise interaction and communication among systems because systems are dynamic and each system of any kind whether a tree, a fly or education is a surviving system and is in a process of energy dissiptation for its own survival.

Teaching is such a system having the potentials and drawbacks of any other system that needs to put up a fight for its survival to achieve the intrinsic goal for which it is designed. Because of the unique importance of this systemic perspective, I have employed it as my starting point. Systems approach enables us to move right into the intrinsic structure of teaching as a system, undertake an analytic operation, know its full potentials, lay bare the fundamentals at work within this system, spell out the problems that lie hidden and tap the resources that lie equally hidden and untapped so that this system comes handy in our endeavour to develop the personality of the learner in the classroom. The subsystems of (a) the learners, (b) the teacher, (c) materials and aids, (d) information and skills, and (e) the interaction among these subsystems, intelligent, creative and mechanical have great roles to play in achieving the goal.

3. Teaching an Organization of Techniques

Teaching is essentially a system. By this we are not depriving 'teaching' of all its significant functional and process components. As we shall see later the word system is used here not purely in its structural sense but inclusive of all process and functional perspectives. Teaching is not only a system but a well-organised system, only that we fail to perceive the organisation and the order as transparently as we should. The purpose of this present monograph is to lay bare before the teaching community this organisation and enable our teachers belonging to all disciplines organise their teaching practices with greater integrity and effectiveness. Most teachers fail as effective teachers precisely because they fail to perceive and use the great potentials of this system which we call teaching.

If teaching is a system it has three fundamental aspects, what we shall call (a) *Approaches*, (b) *Procedures*, and (c) *Techniques*. A teacher belonging to any discipline goes into the classroom well equipped with, first, an approach. All approaches are axiomatic with a set a fundamental principles at its core. He has a definite theory on hand. This is not, at this level, any theory of pedagogy, instead theory forms the remote background of his teaching. The teacher at the time of teaching may not be aware of this theory. But all his proximate practices which are our immediate concern in this paper spring from and are based on this theory. This theory will belong to a fundamental discipline to which the particular discipline he is teaching is related. In most cases this theory will belong to (a) psychology, (b) Sociology, (c) Linguistics, or (d) general education. This theory which constitutes the first constituent of the teacher's approach to teaching and determines and directs remotely what he will be doing in the classroom.

The teacher's *approach* to the classroom has a second constituent. This too is a theory, but one more specific, proximate and related than the first component. This theory is strictly pedagogical while the first one was not. This theory consists of a general pedagogical framework specifically part of the discipline the teacher is teaching. This tells the teacher how he should go about in dealing with that particular discipline.

In the case of, for instance, English Language Teaching the first component may be a theory of psychology and the second component of the teacher's approach may be, say for instance, structural approach.[1]

The second fundamental aspect of teaching is the *classroom method*. While approaches are axiomatic, all methods are procedural. The theories that we have talked about provide the remote directions to the teacher's work in the classroom whereas the classroom methods narrow down the entire thing to a *framework* within which the teacher will function. Again, more specifically, a method is an immediate guideline or framework within which the teacher belonging to any discipline or in any sort of classroom organises his teaching devices in the classroom. This aspect of teaching called classroom method specifies in English Language Teaching, for instance, the framework for the teaching of grammar, vocabulary or reading. A particular method specifies the teaching of grammar in one way while another method recommends a different organisation of the classroom activities.

The third aspect of teaching as a system is the *classroom technique*. While approaches are axiomatic, methods procedural, techniques are implementational. Equipped with a remote and a proximate set of principles, and employing a procedural framework the teacher enters the classroom to do his work. As a well prepared practitioner he employs one teaching device after another. Each of these devices we call classroom techniques. These are well defined and systematic activities that the teacher initiates from time to time to induce activities among the learners. These are not casual or random actions done by him. All classrooms of any kind requires narration, explanation or description of a given thing. We call this device a classroom technique. Questioning is another technique. Pictorial illustration is a third. In otherwords, these are the concrete things that the teacher does in the classroom to initiate learning.

4. Lecture: Aspects and Techniques: Introduction

In recent days it has become a fashion to condemn lectures outright and at the same time those who tend to do this resort only to the lecture method most unscrupulously. The essential role the lecture method plays in university teaching cannot be overlooked. Inspite of its inadequacies lecture stands as the most basic teaching method in this context. The cynical attitude that people have towards lecture is based on the misconception that lecture is a 'one-way method' with no potentials for the much appreciated classroom interaction. But this is a much misconceived approach to the lecture method. Lecture has great potentials and there is no other method that can ever substitute lecture as the most basic teaching procedure in University teaching. The following pages will examine what techniques can, in fact, make lecture a most effective classroom procedure at the university level.

5. The Role of Questioning in Lecture

One of the most effective ways of converting a lecture into a fruitful "exercise is to employ *intermittent questioning*. Questioning should form part of a lecture as a curb to its 'fire-brand' nature. Here we are trying to combine two very basic classroom techniques into one procedure. These are 'narration and questioning'. The lecture method is basically *narration* that will signify what we usually call *explanation* or *description*. It is because of the one-way direction of the narrative techniques that is the very core of the lecture method that it lacks the necessary classroom dynamisms and hence the criticism it stands. The first thing necessary, therefore is to combine narration and questioning in lecture. Lecture can have two kinds of questions combined to it. (i) *reflective questions* and (ii) *genuine questions.*

The teacher amidst speaking by way of explanation or description stops and asks a question. This is done not with a view to obtaining an answer from the students by way of information, but to help the students think and reflect upon a point that the teacher is making. No answer is expected here; the purpose is merely to elicit interest and mentally attempt answers by the students. Genuine questioning on the other hand expects answers from the students. This is not for eliciting merely thinking but to involve the students in the teaching- learning process and often to add to the information that the teacher is trying to give. The questions need to be short, well-structured and lucid so that they do not take away the student's attention from the points that the teacher is making. The questions should therefore be closely linked to the narration. The questions can be based on the material that the teacher has just presented or on the matter that will at once follow.

By and large questioning serves a number of purposes: 1. Questioning keeps the students alert and holds their attention. 2. Questioning links various aspects of the lecture and helps the students keep trace of as well as view the whole lecture in a unified manner. 3. Questioning functions as a revision technique amidst a lecture and helps the students to consolidate and retain the content of the lecture. 4. Lastly, questioning adds interest and variety to teaching and helps the students genuinely participate in the teaching - learning process.

6. The Use of the Chalk-board

Apart from questioning that forms an integral part of lectures, there are other techniques that have similar functions to perform. The *chalkboard* is the most important among these. It is true that chalkboard is an anathema for many teachers' dignity to turn to the chalkboard and use it for any purpose. But it has been recognised that the chalkboard is the most basic teaching aid that is at the disposal of all teachers at all levels. The chalkboard serves a number of effective purposes in course of lectures: 1. A lecture, basically as a narrative technique, provides only an audio-lingual modality for the students to hang on. The chalkboard comes to the rescue to provide a fundamental visual effect parallel to the narration. 2. This visual effect can come in the form of central points of the narration, the key terms (names, labels, difficult words) that are employed in the lecture, jottings of various kinds, illustrations, and sketches that form part of the lecture.

Again the chalkboard (5) helps the slow-learner group in the class trace the lecture points while taking down notes. This is a very important aspect of lectures. There are three different major groups in a class (See Sec. 12). These groups will respond to the lecture only in three different ways. There is a considerable gap between the responses of 'the motivated bright learner group' and 'the unmotivated slow learner group.' Between these extremes the response varies considerably. If the lecture does not in any way take care of this reality as it is the beneficiaries of the lecture will be limited only to the first group. Again the chalkboard comes to the rescue. Working on the chalkboard puts a break to the actual narration, slows down the pace of the work and this in turn enables the slow learner group to keep pace with the lecture. Again, the presentation of the key points on the chalkboard helps this group organise themselves much better to come to grips with the matter discussed.

Lastly, (6) the chalkboard helps the teacher present the whole content of his lecture in a well-organised nutshell as the proceeds with the lecture, and at the same time consistently refer back to the points already discussed. Referring back in this manner would be greatly helpful to all groups in the classroom. This works as a consolidation, review as well as recover the points that the students lose track of. In otherwords the chalkboard is the most handy aid that the teacher can spontaneously turn to.

7. Presentation of the Lecture Points

Lectures can be made most effective by a systematic presentation of the lecture points. People are sore about lectures at large chiefly because teachers often make it a haphazard affair. Talking whatever just comes to one's mouth does not become a lecture. A good lecture is a painstaking, scientific and well-organised activity. No amount of preparation can leave a teacher totally complacent at the time he delivers the lecture. All lectures call for continuous and on the spot organisation of the content matter. Since lectures can never be a commit-to-memory affair, as the exposition is in progress the teacher is called on to organise and reorganise, elaborate and cut short the material that he is presenting.

The lecture points can be presented in a number of ways. First, it can be done through *handouts*. This is perhaps the most sophisticated and effective way of presenting the lecture points to the students. The handouts which are duplicated for the specific purpose contain the material of the lecture presented as general outline, detailed points or as sketches of a variety of kinds. The chief advantage of the handouts is that the students need not have to take down the material in a half-hearted, haphazard way. They are available to the students in the original way the teacher has conceived of the material. This organisation can be upset while the students take down notes in their own incompetent way. These handouts are of great help to those for whom note-taking is impossible. The lecture consequently turns out to be fruitful to them through these handouts.

Second, the lecture points can be presented on the *chalkboard* at the very beginning. While the preparation and distribution of handouts involve time, labour and cost, the use of the chalkboard is most handy. Beginning a lecture with the presentation of the lecture points on the chalkboard is a very effective method of doing it. The teacher will come fully prepared with the plan of the lecture. He presents the material in three main ways: 1. In a sequence of *points* worked out as single words, phrases or a simple sentences. 2. In a *sketch or diagram* that enables the students to trace the whole lecture as it will be in progress as well as see the whole scheme in a nut-shell. 3. In a sequence of *questions* presented on the chalkboard so that the whole lecture will be organised around the content matter of these questions.

The lecture points can be presented on the chalkboard also in a simultaneous manner. Instead of presenting the whole scheme of the lecture right in the beginning, the scheme is developed gradually as the lecture is in progress. The scheme gets unfolded again in a number of ways: 1. Through *points* worked out as single words, phrases or short sentences. 2. Through a *sketch or a diagram* that is gradually worked out. 3. Through *questions* that are presented one after another. As the lecture progresses these points or scheme gets worked out on the chalkboard. One may also visualise a presentation of the lecture points on the chalkboard on completion of the lecture. But this may not be so effective as the former two. All the same wherever the teacher cannot present the scheme in the beginning or simultaneously, he should try the possibility of presenting the points towards the end of the class.

Third, the lecture points can be most effectively presented through an *overhead projector*. This is perhaps technologically the most advanced way organising a lecture class. The use of the T.V., Video, or films cannot become a regular feature in everyday classrooms. But the potential of the overhead projector as a technological aid to lecture is most widely recognised. The overhead projector can be a handy device that can become part of the everyday classroom. The teacher works out the lecture material into a sequence of *well-organised points, a diagram* or into a sequence of *questions*. The scheme is then transferred onto (a) *transparencies* or (b) the assotape (cellulose tape).

The use of the overhead projectors at the time of a lecture makes a world of difference to the efficiency of the lecture. First of all we are thereby combining two modalities into one operation: the *visual* and the *auditory* modalities. The slow learner group of the class can easily catch up with the work; the average learner group will benefit most from this method; and the bright learner group will find the work unusually challenging. The use of the overhead projector enables the teacher to present before the class sketches and diagrams (either commercially available or self-prepared) which otherwise becomes impossible to use in the classroom. The teacher himself finds it very useful as he has something definite to hand on in course of the lecture.

In short, lectures can be made most productive, effective and interesting through the use of 1. handouts, 2. chalkboard, and 3. overhead projector. A regular use of any of these or the combination of the three one way or other can considerably alter the general impression that people have of lectures. Whatever device we may use, a systematic presentation of the content of the lecture either through points, diagrams or questions will remain the chief way of making the best out of the lecture method. This makes the talk concrete, perceptible, immediate, well-organised and tangible. This at the same time takes care of the heterogeneous structure of every class that the teacher might encounter.

8. The Role of Organisation in Lectures

Another factor that makes lectures usually less effective and uninteresting is the lack of intrinsic organisation or internal coherence. Making a lecture a well-organised and well-documented presentation of the most relevant information with minimum redundancy is not at all an easy task. Yet it is this characteristic that lies at the core of an effective lecture. The language that is used as the medium has a great role to play in communicating the quantum of information to the students. The various aspects of presentation controls the student's response to the lecture. But the total effect of the lecture with respect to (i) the reception, (ii) retention and (iii) recall depends very much on how well the points of the lecture are organised.

What exactly is organisation in a lecture ? Is organisation only a total effect, or is it systematically analysable ? I have called organisation 'the internal coherence' of the lecture. The lecture is in fact a discourse that has several purposes to serve the main purpose being the communication of a given quantum of specialised information. In a discourse we are employing a large number of linguistic and communicative strategies or devices to put across either in speech or in writing a quantum of information or a degree of intension to make it a successful affair. Lecture being a discourse presented through the modality of speech we find the linguistic and communicative strategies clearly in operation.

Organisation first of all means these strategies which render a lecture its necessary texture and colour. This means using the language, say

English, according to its discourse devices: correct articles, conjunction's, prepositions, pronouns, reflexives, auxiliaries and correct stylistic choice of words. But at the level in which we are considering organisation it means something different. Taking the linguistic and communicative strategies for granted we focus on the content matter. The content matter is the semantic structure of the discourse i.e., the lecture in the present content. The content matter calls for an inherent coherence. The teacher strictly controls his thought pattern i.e., the stream of his thinking. This calls for long years of practice and considerable restraint. Those who know 'now enough' should stretch the thought stream in deeper analysis to meet the requirement; those who know 'too much' and feel like presenting everything need to exercise great restraint not to confuse far too many issues.

Organisation means thus, controlling the thought stream. The listeners will at once feel that the teacher is 'organised', that he is not 'going wild' and that he picks-up thread even when diversions become necessary. The students are in a position to have a retrospective view of the content matter at a single stretch and at the same time have a crude prospective view of what the teacher will be talking about within the framework of the topic. Organisation, again, means the fundamental sequence: *generatics* are placed in the beginning and thus the topic is introduced. Following these the teacher introduces specific sub-topics. A lecture that involves any kind of explanation, description or exposition (all of which we have put under the label narration) needs to follow one way or other the sequence from generalities to specificities. These sub-topics or aspects are sequenced out in terms of their priorities.

A number of principles are followed in structuring the necessary sequence of the specific sub-topics. 1. The selection of the points must be done with respect to the level of the students, their immediate background, and the scope of the topic in relation to the time allotted to the completion of the topic etc. 2. Points that are redundant and repetitive are avoided. 3. Only those sub-topics are selected that retain the necessary link with the preceding sub-topic. Or else the randomness affects the student's reception and response. 4. As the sub-topics are sequenced and organised a scheme either emerges or the sequencing follows a previously provided scheme. 5. The sub-topics can be ordered into some kind of a diagram that proves most useful to the students. All these aspects render organisation a central role in lecture.

9. Suffixing Lectures with Groupwork

Another technique that would save lectures from getting less effective is to combine lectures with groupwork. This combination does not become feasible where the teacher has only a single period on hand. This combination becomes feasible and most effective in cases where two consecutive periods are available or where the teacher considers two periods which belong to two different days as one unit. The benefits of group activities or group work is unquestionable. All the same lectures and groupwork cannot substitute one another because each has its distinct role to play in teaching.

The most ideal situation is where lecture can immediately be followed by groupwork. As mentioned above this may be done in consecutive or separate periods without too many days' gap between the two periods. Groupwork helps the students bringdown to this level topics that are discussed by the teacher in his lecture. To many who belong especially to the average and the slow learner group the lecture leaves several questions unanswered. If no follow up activity is undertaken these problems will permanently remain unsolved. Groupwork thus functions as a very adequate follow up activity and helps students get this problems solved and points clarified. This factor links lectures with groupwork in a fundamental manner.

Groupwork, again, enables the students simplify through discussion theoretical aspects that the lecture presents. Such theoretical and abstract will be made concrete and brought down to earth when discussed in groupwork. What the teacher presents from his own scholarly perspective and through a framework that is developed from that perspective will now be presented and understood from a more concrete perspective of students themselves who are now involved in a process of understanding the points of the lecture. The teacher too gets an occasion to explain things more in detail while the groupwork is on as he can move about from one group to another.

When groupwork follows a lecture the effect of the lecture becomes fourfold. The two constitutes the most natural combination. A groupwork without a preceding lecture will tend to be empty of content and often a futile exercise. The students need matter to discuss, unless the groupwork is 'language - oriented' and purely meant for language practice. Similarly a lecture without having an opportunity to discuss things often tends to be much less effective and the response too stereotyped. A student who otherwise finds it difficult to ask a question or clarify a point will more easily take part in the discussion and contribute his mite. The topic chosen for the groupwork should not be unrelated to that of the lecture. The close link established between the lecture and the groupwork will prove the combination to be most effective, creative and purposeful.

10. Dictation of Key Sentences as Part of the Lecture

This is yet another aspect that makes lectures more effective. However, slow-paced a lecture may be note-taking becomes a difficult affair for most students. Even intelligent students find it cumbersome to follow a lecture systematically and take down notes without the aid of any visual diagram. Note-taking is again a sub-system as part of academic activities which requires careful training. It is important to see that an excellent lecture in a regular classroom on a regular syllabus item loses a high degree of its utility unless the students are in a position to carry home their own class notes or handouts. A few lines taken down systematically will be more beneficial than a whole lot of material listened to. This is true more from the view point of examinations.

Hence the need for providing a few things dictated. As the lecture is in progress the teacher can stop at a central point and dictate to the students a few sentences that will explain that particular point. This is significant when we see how a part of a lecture becomes less effective or totally useless when students miss this central point of a sub-topic. To ensure that n student actually misses this point of the content matter the teacher dictates a few sentences. Within a holistic viewpoint of lectures a minor aspect of this kind has a place and the teacher needs to be aware of it. The detailed modus operandi of this dictation can be worked out by individual teachers themselves.

11. How to Prepare a Lecture

Lastly, the systems analysis of teaching through the lecture method takes us to the consideration of how to prepare a lecture. A very detailed discussion of how to prepare a lecture can be undertaken; but we shall for present purposes look at only the essentials. The teacher has different attitudes towards lecture as far as preparation is concerned. Some do not consider is necessary at all to spend extra-class hours to prepare themselves while others planout all the details of every class they are expected to engage, with additional on the spot reading for the purpose. Between these two extremes we have a large variety of attitudes to the questions of preparing a lecture.

Teaching through the lecture method involves two levels of preparation: 1. remote preparation as well as 2. immediate preparation. Remote preparation on the basis of the teacher's education, training and background involves several things. First, the teacher has to work thoroughly on the syllabus which offers the outline of the course on which his lectures will be based. The teacher puts in intensive groundwork when he begins teaching the course for the first time. This is the time when he does a wide-range of reference to find enough material to develop and elaborate upon the syllabus items. He makes detailed notes at this level. The source material that he may utilise for these detailed notes are: 1. main source books and references, 2. notes that he must have prepared in relevant areas, and 3. if available the comprehensive material that he may have in store from his student days when he obtained his basic degree in the subject.

The teacher prepares the groundwork so comprehensively that he is well-acquainted with the most fundamental aspects of the area which the particular syllabus focuses. Once this is done the next important, step is to keep abreast to the latest trends and developments by reading the most recent journals and books. This is not usually done by several teachers, and this knowledge of the subject does not progress from where it was at the time of this education. It requires a higher degree of academic motivation to take all the trouble to keep pace with advancements in one's area of specialisation.

The second aspect of the teacher's preparation for the lecture consists in the immediate preparation. There are several ways of doing this. It all depends how systematic the teacher can be. There are those who go right into source or text books in search of materials immediately before every lecture. This is a poor way and most uncertain way of preparing a lecture. Can one be sure of doing this before all our classes? Such teachers will have nothing on hand to teach in busy times when he cannot sit down and take notes from books. The teacher who needs to be sure of all his classes undertakes a division of work that ensures the topic and the sub-topics for every individual class. In otherwords he keeps the syllabus item neatly distributed in an approximate way with sub-topics for every class. He also develops a system of keeping detailed lecture points and can have resource to these points immediately before his class. He develops a system where he knows exactly where to look for material for his immediate lecture. This can be done through a regular workbook, diary or notes.

A preparation of the kind envisaged above alone can ensure effective teaching through the lecture method. Both the remote and proximate components of the teacher's preparation are unavoidable. The remote preparation is a continuous thing that makes sure of his scholarship in the area of his specialisation. This scholarship is something that every college and university teacher cannot afford to neglect and effective teaching primarily depends on this. The proximate preparation is similarly the only way to ensure the aspect of the inherent organisation of the lecture that we discussed in a preceding section. This would all mean a single-minded concern for and dedication to one's area of specialisation. Even the best prepared teacher can get lost in a lecture class and go totally disorganised leaving the students only a confusion. A thorough understanding of what one is teaching will certainly be of help in picking threads on such occasions and save the lecture from being uneffective.

12. Lectures and the Structure of the Class

The success of a lecture depends also on yet another factor: meeting the heterogeneous structure of every class. Every class of any background or of any level consists of a heterogeneous structure. However small the class may be this factor is applicable to it too. The class consists of a number of groups and sub-groups. First, there is what we shall call, the bright learner group; then the average learner group and lastly the slow learner group. The bright learner group consists of students who are intellectually gifted and are capable of high level performance. The average group constitutes the mean, and has the maximum members who can not be distinguished for this intellectual gifts. The last group consists of students whose performance is relatively poorer than of the former groups. We do not call them 'dull' because each of them may be gifted for performance outside the classroom such as, say, sports or a variety of other skills. These three have further sub-groups whose performance is controlled by the level of motivation. We have the motivated and unmotivated bright learners, the motivated vs unmotivated average learners, and the motivated vs unmotivated slow learners. The lack of motivation brings the performance of every sub-group down to the next lower group.

Teaching through lecture method cannot neglect this structure of the class. Adjusting one's teaching exclusively to any one group is detrimental to the performance of groups. This factor makes classroom teaching exceptionally difficult. One way that is usually resorted to is the group method of teaching. But that can only partly solve the problem. Lecture being what it is the teacher himself has to find a way out. There can be several approaches to this problem. The lecture aims as usual at the largest group: the average learner group. The teacher then introduces elements of adjustment directed to the bright learner group. This may be in the form of more technical language, additional or detailed material or posing more challenging questions. This will provide greater satisfaction and involvement to the brighter group.

Similarly, the teacher introduces elements of adjustments directed to the slow learner group. This may be in the form of less technical language, simpler explanation, greater use of the chalkboard, the use of the handouts as well as questions of less challenging nature which should be answered only by the slow learner group. These adjustments are basic to an effective lecture and the teacher at the time of the lecture should be aware of the need to make and adjustments either ways. These techniques and many more than can be envisaged will indeed make lecture an effective method of classroom teaching. What lies behind all these is an endeavour to be scientific and systematic in the teacher's approach to teaching. A systematic understanding of teaching will take the teacher a long way ahead in his classroom practices.

Notes

1. *Structural Approach* : Structural approach is a body of knowledge that advocates a way of teaching English as a second language. SA advocates that teaching English can most effectively be done through the functional teaching of the grammatical structure of the language. Hence its emphasis on the 'structural syllabus.' Teaching English in India has officially accepted a modified structural approach as its basis.

2

GROUP METHOD IN TEACHING

1. Group Method and the Classroom

The *group method* of teaching has assumed a unique role in present-day classroom practices and it is no wonder that this has become a catch-word of the day. Any method is defined as the overall classroom procedure within whose framework the teaching techniques are organised. The foremost aim of the teacher in the classroom is to organise most effectively a given set of learning experiences which functions as the medium for communicating to the learner a quantum of information or developing in the learner a particular skill. In general education the whole thing is defined in terms of a change in the learner's behaviour pattern.

Group method becomes unique primarily because all other classroom methods presumably aim at the individual learner and establishes chiefly a one-way contact with the learner. The following characteristics make the group method of teaching in many ways unique. Any form of group method *directly involves* the learners not merely in responding to the techniques that the teacher employs but the learner becomes an integral part of the procedure. The very term 'group' means that *a unit* is organised within the framework of the classroom, that consist of a given number of students chosen by the teacher. The group is called a unit because of a specific purpose that is attached to its formation over and above the overall purpose for which the class as a whole is organised. This specific purpose renders the group a unique unit within the framework of the classroom.

Group method thus calls on the learner to *reorganise the class* into a feasible number of such smaller units as mentioned above. In the regular class the teacher seldom focuses attention on the texture the whole class. His attention is focused on the content matter of his lesson on which his teaching is organised. The moment the groups are formed the teacher's attention shifts from where it used to be into this structural unit which we have called a group. This shift in attention is a very significant aspect of all group work and makes this method all the more important as a method of teaching. The teacher makes up his mind as to how many groups the class should be divided into. The number of groups he forms depends very much on the type of group activity he intends to undertake. Certain type of language work can best be done in smaller groups or even in pairs, while certain other type of language work requires larger groups.

The Group method of teaching becomes unique, again, because hereby we are putting into practice the most advanced and highly valued principle of teaching: *the learner involvement* in the learning experiences organised by the teacher. Here is a method which not only provides the optimum learner involvement and opportunity for the principle 'do and learn' but also leaves the real *responsibility* for the activities to the learner himself. As we shall see in detail later, the group as a unit with a specific purpose is entrusted with a task and with all the responsibility for working out the task. In other words group method becomes highly task-oriented. By the very nature of the task on hand any form of group method assumes a communicative characteristic, as the task is carried out not by the individual in isolation but by the group as a unit based on mutual communicative interaction.

Group method thus is *task-oriented* and inherently *communicative* by nature. The teacher conceives of the group as a unit only with reference to a task. A task is some kind of an activity pre-conceived and pre-designed by the teacher. It cannot be anything random to make the whole affair productive. In other words the teacher who intends to undertake group work needs to be fully prepared. The teacher of English, for instance, has to have on hand a definite task to get some language item, some structure or vocabulary, practised in the group in a communicative manner. Group method transfers the onus of work from the teacher's mouth to the nucleus of the group. This transfer is what is envisaged most by all contemporary thinkers in education because this is what guarantees concrete and productive learning in the classroom. This transfer of work from the teacher to the group with the teacher's role shifted to that of a guide and supervisor is rooted in the basic structure of group method as a most advanced method of classroom teaching.

Group method calls for a dynamic and creative teacher who can yoke the group into very purposeful tasks. It does not mean that group method can be employed only by the most intelligent and resourceful teachers. If this is so, then all the dynamism of the method as such is diminished. The very method is most resourceful and thus a less resourceful teacher can initiate the group method of teaching into his or her classroom with proper guidance. Group method requires planning and preparation, perhaps a greater degree of planning than a regular class calls for. All the same the difference is that any form of group work in which the students are yoked into some form of task and are guided to undertake some form of work, by itself guarantees effective learning. This would mean that group method is a self-guaranteed classroom procedure and the degree of effectiveness depends on the concreteness and feasibility of the task given to the group and its link with the objectives of a teaching unit for which the group method is employed.

2. Group Method for the Bright Learner

Group method is primarily conceived of in order to meet several of the problems related to the structure of the classroom. The classroom is inherently heterogeneous. This would primarily mean that what the classroom contains is not a simple, homogenous group. Any class, however advanced or however elementary, consists of three major groups: 1. the bright learner group, 2. the average group, and 3. the slow learner group. These three groups are further divisible into sub-groups on the basis of the level of the learner's motivation. Thus we have in the class the range between the motivated bright learner group on the one extreme, and the unmotivated slow learner group on the other.

The three groups which any class consists of is the basis of all the heterogeneity that the teacher has to deal with while teaching and which most often defeats his purpose because of the influence this heterogeneity exerts on the performance of the class Group method is unique solution that comes to the teacher's help to deal effectively with this problem. First, the teacher has to deal with the legitimate problems of the bright learner group of his class. Let's examine what these problems are and how effectively he can deal with these. The *bright learner* in the class has a few legitimate demands to make. He is intelligent, resourceful, creative and understands things much quickly. He is capable of responding to the teaching stimuli with greater speed, ease and ingenuity. But most often all the work that goes on in the class is directed to the average group which occupies the bulk of the class. This leaves him with less or no challenge and he is left to mind his own business. The teacher's attitude often has a snubbing effect on this bright mind. His problems are therefore unique.

Group method comes to the rescue of the bright learner. The primary reason for this is the responsibility and sense of initiative attached to the group method which the bright learner group can easier make use of. The following aspects make group method the most adequate procedure to cater to the bright learner's needs. This group is quick in comprehending the work done in the class. Through group method the teacher ensures the presence of these bright students in all the groups that he forms for a given task. Depending on the number of such students available the teacher takes care to distribute these students to lead all the groups. The quick comprehension ability that these students are capable of is tapped under these circumstances. A task the teacher presents to the groups for their perusal is at once understood by these students in all its detail. They at once function as the mediators between the teacher and the other members of a particular group in making them properly understand the task on hand.

The teacher employs group method to bias his work towards the bright learner group. This is done as a conscientious activity. The group are formed in such a way that every group contains one or more bright students. Adequate instructions are given to these students in order to lead the group activity with greater ease. When group work is biased towards the bright learner group the teacher choses an area of activity considerably above the level of the average group so that a degree of challenge is thereby provided to this group which in turn leads the whole class to the task assigned. The group rests with the bright student who acts as the leader. By providing this opportunity and creating such an environment the teacher is catering to the needs of the bright learner group in according with the most valued principles of teaching. On the other hand the teacher is directing the potentials and resources of this affluant group towards; the less privileged and helps these students to draw profits and enhance their learning experiences. Group method is found to be a rare method in which this can easily be achieved. The teacher has to be careful about the choice of the group activity to achieve this aim, and provide guidance in such a manner that the bright student does not feel any degree of pampering or interference in leading the activity of the particular group.

3. Group Method for the Average Group

After the bright learner group, the teacher's attention is focussed on the average group which constitute the bulk of the class. In fact every teacher without any conscious effort directs his teaching to this particular group since this constitutes the majority. There are several features that characterise this group of students. A section of the average group is so highly motivated that this performance equals that of the bright learner group. This is the motivated average learner group. Teachers are delighted by this group because working with them does not call for exceptionally challenging material, they take their own time in completing an assignment, and their enthusiasm can easier be maintained.

Group method as in the case of the bright learner group can take care of the average group in the class. Quits a number of enthusiastic teachers are so aware of the presence of the bright students in the class that in their enthusiasm they tend to provide challenging material and work more often than actually required, Under such circumstances the average group is deprived of their right to work at a lower level and in a slower pace. This is a serious problem that the teacher has to face. The average student requires relatively more explanation, less cumbersome activities, simpler language both at the recognition and production levels, and greater help for their work. It is here that group work comes to the teacher's rescue. At this level the teacher focuses not on the bright learner group but on the average students. The group activities are organised in this context not for the bright but for the average. Both at the levels of the content matter and activities the teacher keeps the average group and its intake abilities in mind.

Group method easily comes to the average student's help. Content matter that he has not partly or fully comprehended can now be explained to him in the group by more affluent students. The question and answers as well as the discussions that are coordinated in the group help the student understand the material in greater depth and enable him to begin thinking independently. It is important to note that the material handled by the teacher has now been brought down to the level of the students to be handled by them at their level. Difficult vocabulary is simplified; structures are naturally made easier, the complexity is levelled into natural simplicity. This may be done often at the cost of some valuable information that the group may miss in the course of such simplification. Such losses can be rectified by the teacher if he makes it a point to move, from group to group and ensures satisfactory work as planned by him. While the group method of teaching provides challenges to the bright learner, this method helps the average student have better intake of the work done in the regular class.

4. Group Method for the Slow Learner

The slow learner poses unique problems in the classroom. Many are prone to call this 'dull students.' We are using the term slow learner as he is not dull in any sense of the term and he can be exceptionally bright in a skill-oriented course, or he could be a fine sportsman. We have called him slow because he is too slow to comprehend academic matters, too slow to respond to academic stimuli and slow in relating any theoretical matter to its practical corollary. It is such a group of students that the teacher is expected to handle and teach in the classroom; and this becomes a constant headache for any conscientious teacher.

The group method comes as an answer to many a problem posed by the slow learner group. We have seen that this group too slow to comprehend academic matters. When a slow learner is put in a group which consists of both the bright and the average students this becomes a unique environment for him to comprehend things much faster. The teacher's pace is usually too fast for him to follow and this causes a degree of depression in him. This happens even in the case of those teachers who make efforts to reach out the slow learner group. For those who do not make such attempts the slow learner's world in the classroom becomes a lost world.

Group method helps the learner in several ways. The content matter discussed or the task worked out in the group makes a world of difference to him. He *receives* things at his own pace now because his own peer group is working on the material. The close-knit character of the small group as a unit helps greater *interaction*. The members feel greater freedom to express themselves. There is a sense of being proximate to all that is going as against the remoteness that is often created by the regular class. Against all this background the slow learner comprehends things with greater ease.

Group method on the other hand creates such an atmosphere in which the slow learner can *communicate* himself with greater ease. In the regular classroom he is incapable of giving responses or of taking participation in the regular work because he is slow to comprehend and to communicate. Group method allows him the necessary freedom to talk to the other members. Just as the teacher biased his groupwork to the bright and the average student, he must now bias the work to the slow learners of the class. While providing guidance and while supervising the teacher should himself be aware the objective on hand.

5. Techniques in Group Method

We have labelled the present manner of teaching in the classroom as 'group method' because of its characteristic as a classroom procedure. As a procedure which the teacher is employing at a given class hour to get a quantum of work done; group method consists of any number of *techniques*. The techniques that the teacher employs defines from time to time as part of his overall classroom procedure and controls the student's response. Hence the choice and organisation of these techniques of group method are very important and controls the effectiveness of the procedure.

Any technique that the teacher chooses for the group work should have the following characteristics: 1. The particular techniques should enable the whole group *to work as a team*. If the whole thing comes down to individual students sitting down and merely writing down answers to questions then the very purpose of group method is defeated. 2. The Particular technique should help every individual student to have *a share of the work* and contribute his mite to the work of the team. The leader of the group should not become another monopolising substitute for the teacher. 3. The particular technique should *generate activity* because all group work is in some way or other task-oriented. The pupils should get down to some form of work. The particular technique should have a *fundamental link* to other techniques that precede or follow. 5. The technique chosen for the activity should be one suitable for *practice or materials production* and not meant for introducing new ideas or language items or for any form of evaluation. The teacher may have on hand the following pool of techniques for organising group work:

1. ***Interquestioning***: Questions is a classroom technique which is used and initiated by the teacher with a view to obtaining answers from students. The teacher's questioning is meant to trigger off some form of activity in the class. Interquestioning is the activity of questioning done by the students themselves. This can be done in a regular class and for present purposes, in group work. The teacher needs to pave the background for and provide the material necessary for undertaking this group activity. As group activities are meant to follow regular classes and the regular presentation of some content matter, the students are in a position to understand the teacher now provides each group with *a list of questions* for use. These questions in one way or other should be accessible to all the members of the group. Once the group is formed the teacher gives the necessary instructions and provides them with the list of questions

The group leader is instructed to co-ordinate the groupwork. The technique of interquestion is applied when one student spells out the first question and the group as a team applies their mind in developing the correct response. It is in doing this that the team makes use of their creative resources. This trial and error process takes them through some degree of exchange of language, ideas and points of view depending on the level at which the group method is used. By developing answers to question which may be language-focussed or content-focussed the method enables the students to (a) think independently, (b) probe into fresh aspects and viewpoints of their own, (c) organise their ideas in a logical manner, (d) express themselves in correct language, (e) develop the communicative use of the language, (f) develop the art of exchanging ideas with a sense of sportsmanship, as well as (g) give expression to the need for satisfactory interaction in such a social situation. The teacher is hereby helping the students achieve these and much more. The success of interquestioning as a technique in the present context depends on how coherently the teacher is in a position to guide each group in deeping itself active as well as in communicating through the language and content matter that he has placed at the disposal of the group. I consider interquestioning as a technique most basic to group method.

2. *Dramatisation* :Group work becomes handy for a large variety of classrooms. Language classrooms have found group method most

congenial chiefly for developing language material and for providing practice. Group method becomes handy in Social science classes when it comes to developing a topic for which the teacher has given thinking is considered most useful. Similarly, Physical sciences or natural sciences can apply group method in order to help students develop relevant topics already presented to them, workout practical sessions that follow theory classes, work on projects in a variety of ways that are directly or indirectly related to the particular course. In similar lines group method comes handy for courses in engineering as well medicine.

The technique of dramatisation is most suitable for language classrooms. The potentials of dramatisation is great in this regard. The group is small enough to work on a particular piece of conversation with two, three or four characters figuring in group method aims at individual involvement and dramatisation offers opportunity for it. The very structure of a dialogue is such that individuals are given specific roles. Group method aims at the concrete use of the language and content matter by the participants and dramatisation offers opportunity for it. Group method aims at a coherent and unified activity by the group as a team and dramatisation employs material that is coherent and unified for use by the group.

The teacher either develops a dialogue himself, adopts any material available or for that purpose just uses dialogues that may be on hand in a textbook. He then places the material at the disposal of the group with suitable instructions as to the use of it. Since the language classroom aims at the development of language skills or language material, the use of the dialogue by the pupils meet these aims. If we aim at the practice of oral skills, the group will work on the dialogue orally. It is possible also to move into written work of any specific kind provided the technique of dramatisation is properly employed by the group.

The teacher makes sure that the participants take turn in 'Playing' the roles in the dialogue. Since the material is meant for language practice the dialogue should be used by the group not just once but several times as the time on hand permits. Dramtisation is based on a formal dialogue since the pupils at any level will not be in a position to produce on this own all the language that such a dialogue requires. The best basis for providing such dialogues are handouts which the teacher can easily prepare and distribute to the groups.

3. *Role Play* : The technique of role play often identified with dramatisation, has greater coverage as a technique and can be undertaken in a regular class in a large variety of ways. Role play is currently recognised as a very important technique for the communicative teaching of language. It is more specific and definable than dramatisation with reference to the activities it is capable of generating. The language teacher suggests a specific number of roles for the group to enact. Role play as a technique will be applied where a number of the team either speaks out or reads out the material that depicts a specific character, the material, for instance, can be on related to any occupation such as *a carpenter* or *a doctor* and describes in short what he does on a particular day. Roles of any kind can be taken up for the work; when the role play involves more than one character we are using the technique of dramatisation. Using the role play alterations of pronouns or tenses can be introduced and practised. The most important applications of this technique consists in the functional use of language, where language functions such as 'making an apology' is the focus of work rather than a grammatical category such as 'a preposition'. Role plays make the work communicative by nature.

4. *Picture Description* : As a group technique picture description has great potential. The essence of the particular technique consists in the development of language based on a picture, sketch, diagram or a chart. The presence of a visual stimulus providing visual modality for the students to depend on makes a world of difference to this ability to produce language or any descriptive or narrative material. In the absence such a visual modality in the form of a picture the student has to depend on his imagination for the background on which the language or material has to be based. The teacher presents a picture for the whole class to work on, or different small pictures that are more less thematically related can be given to each group. The group thus works on the common picture or on the individual picture.

Picture description as a group method technique can he undertaken in several ways. The teacher may provide (a) an outline of the content of the picture, (b) a few sentences on what the picture says, (c) a starting sentence for a small paragraph to be developed, (d) a couple of sentences for a story that can be worked out, and (e) points for a dialogue for which the characters may be part of the picture. The teacher workout the mode of work that he wants the group follow. The groups talk, develop sentences, ask questions and find answers on whose basis the paragraph, story or the dialogue can be developed. The group method as we have envisaged helps interaction, discussion and individual involvement while working on the picture. The student's imagination is not unnecessarily taxed because this thinking is directed to the details of the picture and they are not called on to stretch this imagination beyond the limits of the particular picture. The reports of the groups are presented to the whole class and this enables the whole class to get acquainted with all the different paragraphs worked out by different groups and helps the teacher to make the necessary corrections for the benefit of the class.

The technique of picture description need not be language specific. The teaching of social sciences, natural sciences, engineering and medicine can make use of this technique because more than language teaching these disciplines make use of sketches and diagrams. The difference is that the language classroom aims at developing language-oriented material while the other disciplines aim at developing content-oriented material. After the general session with the whole class the groups can be yoked to the task of developing the content matter which the diagrams and sketches represent. Picture description as a group technique can thus be used effectively by any discipline for that mater. The group interaction should be thought of as the core of the work.

5. *Developing Written Discourses* : This group technique is found most useful in the language classroom for teaching written composition or for developing answers to content-oriented questions. Other disciplines can answers to questions, working out discourses of a variety of kinds and for finalising the content matter of very specific topics under consideration. In all these cases what is actually happening is the development of a *written discourse* by the students themselves. The teacher finds out as many sub-areas of the topic or the question under consideration. Each group is entrusted with a sub-area or sub-question and instructions are given for the exact work to be done.

The group leader initiates the discussion. At a lower level discussion means working on very specific sentences. The group is working on a sub-question. Each member makes attempt to construct a specific sentence for the purpose. This means that he is giving expression to his thinking in the language of the medium. The group as a whole is trained to examine the sentence from a variety of view points such as 1. language correctness, 2. content adequacy, 3. the place of the sentence in the whole discourse (beginning, middle, and) 4. some degree of thematic coherence. The group then accepts, rejects or revises the sentence. If accepted these the sentence is recorded in writing, then the group takes up another sentence constructed by another member, examines its adequacy to the extent the group, can, and accepts, rejects or modified it. The work goes on until a sufficiently long paragraph is worked out. After the group work the groups come together to put the paragraphs or discourses together. The teacher gives a final touch to the material prepared and the whole class can now use the whole discourse brought together and organised under the main topic or question. The focus of this technique is not any oral skill, but either written language or organisation of content material as discourses.

6. *Projects Preparation* : The very term 'project' specifies that the technique is something that can easily and effectively go with group method. Preparation of projects has been intrinsic to all aspects of teaching and to all disciplines. A group can easily be yoked to a group-task in the form of a project in which individual students will have something specific to contribute. The term 'project' indicates that task assigned is not part of the regular course in the form of question-answers or composition or discourses of any kind. A project should enable the learner to make inquiries and references outside the main body of the course. A project is related to the course but not essentially part of the course, if not as a project the work ioses its significance as a means to the development of the learner's creative abilities and research potential. A project can be as simple as a small write up under a picture or the preparation of a small model as well as it can be as serious and elaborate as a paper for a seminar or plan for a scheme. Whatever may be its range it has been widely recognised that projects preparation is one of the best methods for training the creative faculties of students.

Projects of very limited scope can be assigned to groups as a task. Each group may be given a book with a specific area marked out for work. In lower classes may be a summary that the teacher aims at while at higher levels it can be a critical review of the original material. The project may be an experiment in science or a small enquiry into some area of geography. It may be the preparation of a map, a model, a diagram or a design. The language teacher can, again, think of an area in grammar for which the groups can be asked to work out exercises.

Teaching material or draw sketches for illustration. Since group work is usually done during a single class period the teacher needs to think of very small projects, or else he may obtain more than one class hour and work at a stretch in groups so that a project can be completed with care. The biggest asset of project technique as par of group method lies in the very concrete and often physical involvement thāt the work offers to each individuals.

7. *Outdoor Activities* : The project method of teaching is not restricted to the four walls of classroom but can be conveniently extended outside the classroom. This way the part enlar method of teaching is applicable to all disciplines which have scope of work outside the regular classroom. Outdoor activities as part of group method cannot be restricted to just one class period and require longer stretch of time. The teacher plans the outdoor activity keeping in mind allow such factors. Outdoor activities as group work can include 1. observation and reporting of events or things, 2. working on a project that needs outdoor activity, 3. preparing drafts of various kinds based on things and events that students can observe in the world outside, and 4. any activity that can be given a concrete task to particular groups but can finally be collated as one single activity.

Out door activities as group method have great potential for language teaching. Observation and reporting of events in the world outside puts the student right in a communicative context and enables him to learn the most sensitive areas of language with reference to concrete life experiences other than merely projected by the textbook. Students do things with greater enthusiasm and inspiration that cannot be made available to them within the four walls of the classroom.

Mention is made only of the most general techniques that can constitute part of group method. The specific ways of implementing these have to be worked out by the teacher depending on the level for which he is planning group work. It is important to see that group method is a very scientific and systemic mode or carrying out classroom teaching. Techniques form the core of group method. The label group method is just an abstraction and like any other method it specifies only an overall procedure. The concrete success of group method depends on what techniques we employ for the procedure. The teacher should be in a position to identify the need and background of the class as a whole on the one hand and re-orient the group tasks to the sub-groups we have already mentioned in the beginning.

The teacher can have a pool of group techniques on hand adequate to the level at which he is working. This pool of techniques comes handy whenever he plans to teach through group method. The language teacher may attach the techniques to the components and skills of the particular language he is teaching. Teachers of other subjects need to tag the techniques to the task they have in mind. The planning has to be done on the basis of the techniques and the material that will go into group work. The choice of these has to be guided by the characteristics and aims of group method as discussed on the proceeding pages.

6. Materials for Group Method

The success in the use of group method for teaching, depends on three aspects: 1. the group techniques, 2. the materials used and 3. the organisation of the group work. The teacher has to be conscious of the importance that materials play in any form of group work. By *materials* in the present context we mean anything which the students depend on for this group work. By nature is given something to work on. This again makes group work unique. In a regular class the teacher can use simple narrative or demonstrative techniques and the class has often a passive role to play with little or no involvement except listening, copying or reading. The moment a group is formed the teacher is giving shape to an independent unit whose members have an aim on hand different from that of the other groups. The small group has a task and feels responsible and involved, and experience which is not usual with regular classroom teaching. This feeling has much to do with the material that the teacher places in the hands of the group.

A large variety of materials can go into group work. In planning, preparing and using such materials the teacher is conscious of all those characteristics that make group method unique, with its potential for interaction, communication and individual involvement. The following categories of materials go into group method of teaching.

1. *A list of questions* which the groups will use interquestioning. The questions will be used also for initiating for discussion in the group or for working on content matter in non-language classrooms. 2. *An outline of a discourse* which the groups will use for initiating discussion and for developing the particular discourse. This may be for an essay, a

short composition, a story, a report or any other discourse. 3. *A substitution table* for the teaching or English or any identical material for other subjects as a frame on whose basis the groups can function and produce sentences in English, as well as content oriented-material for other subjects. 4. *A picture, a sketch or a diagram* which the groups will use for initiating oral work or written work depending on the specific need on hand. The picture substitutes the students's imagination as the basis for the production of the material. 5. *A model* that has a different functions to perform. A perform provides a three dimensional experience and the students can apply this creative faculties in more concrete a manner and this can generate greater interest and enthusiasm. It becomes essentially an experience of transforming non-verbal experience into the modality of language and thus derive greater sense out of the specific learning experience.

A variety of other material too can be envisaged for the task. 6. *An inventory of words* can generate much group activity as these words function as call-words for the features of experience that the words represent. The language teacher can yoke the groups into the construction of sentences which can further be transformed into questions. The members of the group can ask these questions one by one. Since the whole sequence is already worked out on paper, the 'discussion' will be easier and fruitful. 7. *A report* can be put before the groups at advanced levels, and the groups should analyse the content of the report which may pertain to any activity of a formal nature. The groups are asked to produce a report in similar lines relating an activity or of different activities that they have in the school. 8. *Magazines or news paper cuttings* can very well generate group activities. This can be language-specific or content-specific. These paper cuttings and magazines an provide a range of topics for work by students. If these are related to the course under consideration the benefits of the work becomes a fourfold.

Apart from materials that are listed above the teacher can make use of a variety of (a) audio-lingual, (b) visual and (c) audio-visual aids to keep the group engaged. Of these, 9. *Overhead projectors* offer great scope for use in the group method of teaching. The teacher can make use of self-prepared or commercially available transparancies for projecting material for the group. As the overhead projector is equipped with cellulose tape on which outlines, sketches, designs, lists of items as well as language material can be drawn for projection the group can all simultaneously work on one and the same material from a variety of perspectives. 10. *Recorded Material* can offer opportunities for group work in which students will have added interest because of the variety that it can introduce into the work. Just as visual material is presented either on the chalkboard, through pictures or on the overhead projector, audio-lingual material presented on the tape can trigger off group work in a significant manner. A simple tape or cassette recorder can serve the purpose instead of a language laboratory. In non-language classroom such recorded material presented to different groups can easily introduce the content material that is the focus of the particular class. This is especially true when the teacher desires to have a language model better than his own.

Finally, we have (11) *Films, the television and the video.* The role of these, especially of the television and the video cannot be over-stressed. The potential of these for classsroom teaching has been fully recognised. But these too have significant role to play in presenting the material for group work. The use of such audio-visual aids and other technological devices mentioned above are of help in presenting the basic material for duplicated for the groups. The teacher may on the otherhand opt for most simplified mode of preparing and presenting material for group work because complexity in materials preparation and for group work because complexity in materials preparation and presentation must not at any rate prevent the teacher from taping the resources of the group method of teaching in the classroom.

7. Safeguards for Effective Group Work

Group method as a classroom procedure is often misused than used effectively chiefly because the teacher is either not aware of what the whole thing is meant for or has developed a lethargic attitude towards any such innovative mode of teaching. As we have seen, any form of group work should be supervised by the teacher to ensure the best result. What should the teacher look for? What safeguards should he care for to ensure the best results? The techniques, the material and the organisation of group work should be so co-ordinated that the individuals of the group should be able (a) *to think independently*, or make some independent contribution to the group task. If this is not achieved then we shall not reap the rewards the work. The whole thing will merely be a replication of the regular class work. The group should be able (b) *to probe into fresh aspects and view points of their own.* This enquiry by the group is central to group work. The techniques, material and organisation should reflect this particular characteristics of effective group method. The members should be in a position, (c) *to organise their own ideas in a logical manner.* Just as we educate then to think independently we also train the members of the group to organise this ideas with a focus, with a definite orientation and in a definite perspective. Logical thinking is a fundamental aim in the training of young minds. Group method offers ample opportunities for this purpose.

The students should again be able (d) *to express their ideas in acceptable language.* However independently and logically we think, it all becomes uneffective if we do not have on hand the necessary language to express ourselves. Self-expression should not become a suffocating experience for the student. Hence the important of language as the medium of communication. The teacher has to be conscious of the acceptability of the language in which students express themselves while communicating in the group. This leads to an equally important corollary (e) *the communicative use of the language.* Group work at all should enable the learner to acquire the communicative use of the language. The teacher needs to be trained in and be aware of such communicative strategies that makes the student's language most effective.

Group work should be oriented to and ensure the member's ability (f) *to express their ideas and opinions in a spirit of sportsmanship.* Students should be educated to participate in discussions with concern for the ideas and opinions of other so that we are able to accept or criticise the opinions and views of others with considerable generosity. The teacher ensures also the group's ability (h) *to create and maintain an atmosphere of cordiality* in which every participant is given an opportunity to communicate his viewpoints or whatever be the little contribution he has to make. All these safeguards mentioned above are fundamental characteristics of any effective group work. The teacher has to be constantly conscious of these and make attempts to imbibe these into the working of the group. His efforts to coordinate the techniques, the material and the organisation of the group activity to ensure these characteristics will certainly make group method a rewarding experience for the learner who is otherwise lost in an abstract world of the regular classroom.

3

TUTORIALS AND SEMINARS IN THE CLASSROOM

1. The Role of Tutorial System in Teaching

The tutorial method of teaching has long since been a partial answer to the drawbacks of the traditional classroom especially in colleges and universities. All the same hardly any attempt is made to understand its potentials and tap the resources of this method in classroom teaching. Why do the learner, the teacher and the teacher educator constantly look up in wonder not knowing how to deal with the situations that crop up in classroom teaching from time to time? What are these problems? The learner in the classroom finds himself in a precarious position. He ordinarily looks for (a) involvement, (b) alteration in the learning stimuli, (c) interaction with his peergroup, (d) clarity in the teacher's presentation, (e) demonstration of theoretical components in this practical dimensions; (f) departures from the syllabus core to extra learning experiences and so on. In otherwords the student doesnot wish to be a guinea pig submitted to strict physiological conditions, but as we have all the while been stressing, he calls for intelligent manipulation of his learning environment and utilisation of his creative potentials to obtain optimum satisfying interaction with others.

The tutorial system offers considerable opportunities to the students to meet their needs. The lecture method is too formal a system for the students to solve their learning problems. The group method worked out as part of the regular classroom is too narrow to function as this arena for activities that have scope for greater involvement and application. The tutorial system offers opportunities for *a great degree of variety* in the curricular activities. Classes in schools and lectures in colleges are the normal modus operandi of the teaching activity. College teaching makes use of this method with greater feasibility because the system allows its functioning easily. Schools do not experiment with the tutorial system for fear that it will upset the teaching schedule. Tutorial works for several reasons constitute a method of teaching. It is capable of including in its framework a number of sub-methods and techniques of teaching. This framework permits the scope for considerable variety.

2. The Modus Operandi of Tutorial System

Tutorial are attached to regular teaching of the syllabus material. As such a tutorial has a practical function to perform. In college teaching a tutorial is attached to a lecture which takes care of a syllabus unit. At the college level the lecture classes deal mostly with theory while the tutorial takes case of the practical follow-up. The following can be regarded as the possible components of the tutorial system as are envisaged it in the present context :

1. The tutorial method can be organised as *a question answer Session*. The purpose is to initiate interaction, involvement and discussion. Either a topic is introduced in the preceding class or a topic is initiated at the beginning of the tutorial. The teacher takes care to make this introduction short, precise and unambiguous so that the students know what exactly to do during the tutorial. Where the tutorial is attached as a lecture, this introduction can be very short; where the tutorial is held independently, this introduction can be more elaborate. All the same if the tutorial is for a period of forty minutes, this introduction should not exceed, say, five to ten minutes. When a tutorial is held as a question answer session, the teacher has to do the following : (a) provide to the class a set of questions on a handout, or dictate to the class the set of questions they should use for the work. (b) After the introduction the students should take up the questions one by one and should be able to carry on with a full-fledged discussion (question-answer work) with the help of the teacher.

2. The tutorial method can be organised as *a group work session*. Where the question answer session had the whole class together exercising its mind on all the questions and this answers through general discussion, the teacher can employ the group method of teaching as a sub-method within the tutorial. All that we have seen as part of the group method of teaching (monograph.2) is applicable to the present

context. The teacher has to choose the kind of technique that should go into the groupwork. The whole tutorial will now take the form of groupwork and will be concluded if necessary by a general session for the groups to present their answers, findings, or the material.

3. Tutorial can be organised as *demonstration cum discussion*. This is applicable both to language and non-language classrooms. The teacher gives the expository talk, short the precise; then undertakes a demonstration of the relevant aspect of content matter or practice. In the teaching of English this can be the demonstration of situation, a context, a communicative act or a whole set of such context. Demonstration becomes most relevant in non-language teaching classrooms where practical aspects are part of the regular syllabus. Demonstration of any kind which can be done either by the teacher or by one or more students will be followed by discussion. The success of the work depends on the ability of the teacher to coordinate the efforts of the students towards a practical discussion that can look into the various aspects of the demonstration. Demonstration cum discussion as the modus operandi of the tutorial method is most relevant, again, to colleges and departments of education where *skill-oriented teaching* has a major role to play. Tutorial sessions in these institutions have ample demonstrative material to work on. Demonstrations of teaching skills such as questioning, steps of teaching such as the presentation of teaching material, full lessons such as a grammar lesson etc., are part of the material that require demonstration and discussion.

4. *Paper Reading cum Discussion* is a very productive way of organising tutorials. The teacher can choose a relevant topic and help a group of students come prepared with a small paper of the duration of five to ten minutes. The topics may be curricular, co-curricular, or can range from materials recommended for reading by teachers. Each student comes to read the paper after a general expository introduction by the teacher. The reading of the paper is an academic exercise itself and requires the teacher's guidance paper reading has the function of a talk with the help of the written material. Guidance must be needed to make the work an actual presentation. Two or three papers can be read and discussions conducted to ensure right understanding and analysis of the matter.

5. *Discourse Development (oral)* is another productive way of organising the tutorial. Discourse development consists of building oral

material by students with the help of the teacher. It is a very advanced mode of organising a tutorial. This can be done in two ways : 1. keeping the group as a whole and 2. through group meetting. The teacher chooses the topic of the discourse and organises a discussion through very systematically structured questions. Each question refers to a point. On the basis of the student's answer the point is presented on the chalkboard. Out of the forty minutes, the teacher may use, say, twenty minutes for this exercise during which points are developed for a whole discourse. Then using the points on the chalkboard the students will one by one construct the whole discourse orally.

The same can be done in groups using group method. The teacher will in the same manner develop the points on the chalkboard through a process of systematic questioning. Once this work is completed, the tutorial batch will be divided into smaller groups as the teacher finds it feasible. Instead of the whole batch pursuing the matter, the material will now be taken up by individual groups. The members of the particular group develop the whole discourse orally and instead of the teacher guiding the work, affluent participants will make corrections and guide the work. Discourse development (oral) can be both language as well as content matter oriented and is of greater use to the teaching of languages and non-language subjects.

6. *Discourse Development (written)* is yet another method of organising a tutorial. The method is similar to that of discourse development (oral). While the former aims at oral presentation the latter aims at written presentation. The teacher gives the introductory talk and then through a process of questioning organises the discussion. This discussion can continue for about ten minutes. Since more time should be allotted to writing and some kind of followup work, the discussion should be short and well organised. Then the students are asked to write down in well organised form the discourse that have been covered through the discussion. Discourse development (written) is not strictly language oriented; hence I have not used the term 'Composition'. This method can be successful used for developing answers to essay questions for working out reports on practicals, for undertaking revision of materials for regular examinations as well as it is most useful for language work.

7. Tutorial can be fruitfully organise for *developing reference skills.* By reference skills we mean all those academic skills that become necessary for effective use of reference books, dictionaries,

encyclopaedias and other source books (for a comprehensive treatment see Monograph. No. 10). The development of the reference skills is an effective method of organising tutorials both at the school and college levels. The teacher works out the details of the aspects he has to cover for conducting such a session. It is advisable either to make arrangement for the class to sit near the library or have the necessary books brought to the class. In either way the class must have access to reference books and dictionaries. Using concrete examples based on reference sections in books and dictionaries the teacher can give the group training in the use of these source books. Aspects such as : 1. having access to exact reference books, 2. reading relevant sections with a specific purpose, 3. taking notes using a specific methodology, 4. making reference to dictionaries of various kinds, 5. developing a system of filing the materials, notes and relevant information, and 6. developing a system of retrieving the required information and using the information for a specific purpose. Tutorials can be most effectively used in order to develop these reference skills.

8. *Extensive Reading Sessions* can be another manner of organising a tutorial. The importance of reading as an academic skills has to be recognised not only for language teaching but also for other subjects. Extensive reading doesn't mean in this context reading in areas related to the syllabus or reading extra materials of any kind. Extensive reading is used here as a method of organising a reading session which aims at quicker reading, comprehension and analysis of materials which belong to the course such as the textbook, in subjects other than languages. Reading is done in language teaching for its own sake aiming at (a) reading speed and (b) comprehension, which form part of the reading skill. In other areas such as science subjects the specific aim of reading is to *study the content matter* and acquire the information forming part of the reading material. By extensive reading I have meant exactly this kind of reading while the term Intensive Reading is reserved for reading in languages in the classroom. Tutorials can offer considerable scope for conducting such reading sessions to help students prepare themselves for examinations or for acquainting them with new information in a particular field relevant to the course.

9. *Materials Production* constitutes a fruitful mode of organising a tutorial. Tutorial are used for working on the skills of a variety of kinds; tutorials are used for working on the content matter as part of courses.

Tutorial provide equal scope for producing materials. (For details of materials production see Monograph No. 4: workshops). Wherever a course requires production of some material as part of the curriculum, co-curriculuar or extra-curricular activities the tutorial method of teaching can provide scope for it. Materials production is a major part of teacher education courses or courses with practical or skill-oriented bias. Materials production at the level of students can be undertakes as submission tasks, auto-instructional materials and projects of a large variety of kinds (see Monograph No. 5) The teacher plans out in detail the nature and scope of the material that the class should prepare as well as the mode of working it out. The students will be introduced to the work and depending on the nature of the material, the divides the class into groups or keeps the tutorial class together. He should spare at the end enough time to give an overall evaluation of the material or keep this work for a following period. The whole thing trains students in planning and preparing elementary but systematic materials with the definite sense of direction and organisation.

10. Finally tutorials can be organised using *technological devices like the video*. The video has now been envisaged as applicable to the teaching of all subjects and all disciplines. The most significant advantage of the video is its audio visual modality coupled with the facility to manipulate the cassettes at one's will and use it and control it for one's purpose unlike the television. The video with its cue, review, fast movement and freeze facilities are of great classroom application in particular in the teaching of English. A video film can constitute material for organising a tutorial. The teacher chooses the film depending on the subject, area and the topic on which he wishes to work, and shows it to the tutorial group. The films feeds in the material required for the follow-up work. This can be in the form of language work, practice sessions of skills, work on discourses of a variety of types, development of reports, working out answers to questions or preparation of projects for further study and so on. The teacher had a number of things to choose from.

Such is the scope of tutorial system for the classroom. It is a method of academic activity which provide greater albowroom and feasibility for *interaction*, *involvement* and *discussion* than the regular class. The tutorial is conceived of as a avenue for activity and practical work. There is an atmosphere that gives the feeling that the teacher is only an overseer and supervisor and the learning or the activity is undertaken by the class.

The ten areas discussed above constitute the matter for organising the tutorial. Hence these are called sub-methods within the overall method of tutorial work. Tutorial work is conceived of a way of organising teaching as compared to group method, workshop method or project method. Each has something characteristic to contribute to the objective of adding an extra dimension of creativity and purposefulness to the regular and traditional schedule of teaching.

3. Tutorial as Practice-Oriented

Learning can be (a) skill-oriented, (b) task-centred or (c) information centred. In the first case the learner aims at the acquisition of a well-defined skill such as that of a second language. In the second case the learner aims at the competition of a task or an activity which is characterised as involving a number of skills as well as a quantum of information. This is not definable with reference to any one skill as in the case of language learning or typewriting. A practical session in the language laboratory or one in the science laboratory or for that matter the practical sessions in a college of engineering is regarded in the present context as task-centred learning. Information centred learning is what takes place in a lecture class where the teacher aims at conveying a quantum of information on a theory or practice to the class. These three categories of learning cover all academic activities that we may conceive of as related to the classroom.

Tutorials are found to be most adequate method of learning to take case of categories (a). and (b) above. When we say tutorial are practice oriented we mean a number of things :

1. As much as possible tutorials should be used for follow-up work. This would mean that we do not take up a new unit of the syllabus and embark on something that has not in some way been introduced to the students some time or other. A tutorial is not the place to make the class understand a new subject matter. In other words we do not make a tutorial information-centred (category c. above). The most adequate way to use the tutorial session is for the follow-up of some work done in one or the other preceding periods or preceding days. This provides the tutorial a very definite orientation, and differentiates it from regular classes where the teacher works on some new material.

2. A tutorial is the place for showing the class the *practical applications and practical dimensions* of the theory work done in regular

teaching sessions in schools and lecture sessions in colleges. Out of the three groups that constitute a class : the bright learner group, the average learner group and the slow learner group, the second and the third group require greater elaboration, greater illustration or practical applications of several aspects of what we teach in language and non-language subjects. Hence tutorials become necessary to link theory with practice not only in science subjects, but also in arts and humanities.

3. Practice in several contexts means a *form of review* which becomes necessary in the teaching of all subjects. Topics that are covered in regular classes need an avenue for concentrated revision. In all mode of teaching, tutorials can offer with greater ease opportunity to revised such materials. Revision can be done using any of the modus operandi described in section 2 of the monograph. The revision is conceived of here as a very practical dimension of teaching.

4. Practice, in the context of second language teaching, means also *drill of a very organised kind.* A whole tutorial can be yoked to this task where the teacher prepares grounds for oral or written exercises of a variety of kind to ensure mastery of the form, function and meaning of the language item or an aspect of formal grammar. Here the word drill bears a special connotation with a scope wider than what is usually meant in language teaching. Tutorials offer opportunities for a relaxed mode of doing the work to ensure such mastery of the matter as expected. The atmosphere of greater interaction and involvement available at the tutorial becomes congenial for the sort of work we envisage for the practice of a language like English. Tutorials, in short, are practice oriented with greater scope for any form of concrete follow-up work that regular teaching will require. Tutorials offer the time and feasibility for such practical follow-up in a more relaxed atmosphere.

4. Enhansing Student Involvement and Interaction

Tutorials are organised the way they are done primarily to create an atmosphere of student involvement, interaction and thereby elicit meaningful discussion. Classroom interaction has two dimensions : (a) teacher-student interaction and (b) peer interaction. Tutorials aim at tapping both these resources and enhance student participation. The teacher needs to be conscious of this aspect of tutorial method and work with a definite sense of direction. The following guide-lines may be thought of with a view to developing optimum student involvement and classroom interaction.

1. The teacher will aim at organising his work in such a way that the group should continually *feel motivated to ask* questions. It is true that the involvement by the class in the teachers work depends very much on the way be conducts himself. A lecture can become so airy-fairy a thing that the class may feel completely at loss and the least involved. Tutorials are no exceptions to this. Students seldom feel any genuine involvement because of the peculiar atmosphere that is created. The group should feel motivated to stop the teacher, throw a comment, ask a question or make a point. This is the ideal situation; but in all situations the teacher can envisage the group create contexts in which the students will ask a question or make a point.

2. The teacher on his own initiative *asks questions* without leaving the group to take the initiative. On numerous occasions the teacher has opportunities to stop and ask both genuine or reflective questions. In the first case he does not do this but works in such a way that the class feels motivated to say something. It is easier for the teacher to directly ask questions with a view to involving them in the work. The result is that this process sets in motion a habit that helps students talk more freely than otherwise and develop greater confidence in doing this. Every time student asks a question or answers one and correction is made by the teacher, it helps to create much needed language atmosphere for the language classroom.

3. *An attitude or dialogue* with the class ensures a degree of student involvement during the tutorial. The teacher should have the willingness on the one hand and the purposefulness on the other to take the class into confidence. Such an attitude manifested in a number of ways in the teacher's work generates student involvement of a variety of kinds. There can be a big gap created between the teacher and the tutorial class due to the manner in which he speaks, invites questions and conducts himself. A positive bent of mind assumed by the teacher can go a long way in creating an atmosphere congenial to optimum student involvement.

4. *The effective teacher develops a system* of working in the class to keep the learner right at the centre. Only a learner centred approach and not a syllabus or materials centred approach to teaching can the springboard of student involvement in the teacher's work. The teacher being conscious of this need should develop a system which helps him

develop a habit in coordinating student participation. At every given instance the teacher is employing a technique of teaching to initiative work in the classroom. With every technique of teaching he needs to distinguish a dimension of classroom interaction and a way of involving his class in his work. His choice of techniques for the tutorial should place a heavy premium on student involvement. The particular system will emerge to be a bulwark of classroom interaction so far as his teaching is concerned. The system should have components that we have been discussing (also see Monograph 10).

5. Every teacher needs to have a *feedback strategy* that will take care of a high degree of student involvement. The feedback strategy will include all verbal and non-verbal elements that aim at responding to what the students do. Feedback is a continuous thing and the teacher is compelled to give either positive or negative, either verbal or non-verbal feedback of some kind. An effective teacher finds ways to manipulate the opportunities of feedback in so strategic a manner that the whole thing results in student involvement. The teacher has a definite strategy of feedback, in what he says and how he says it to encourage or reprimand the learner. The classroom interaction he generates depends much on this feedback strategy.

For the tutorial to have optimum student involvement the teacher has to have very definite directions on hand. The coordination of the method, the techniques employed, the content matter and the materials used provide him the necessary directions. The teacher's ability in his envisaging the most fruitful way in which this coordination can be realised in his handling the tutorials. A stereotyped attitude to classroom teaching will indeed lack the directions that alone can help him make creative and relevant use of the resources. Student involvement in classroom teaching is an aim itself as well as a component of any effective methodology. The right coordination of the components of the tutorial method will certainly result in providing successful learning experiences without the feeling of alienation on the part of the class.

5. The Place of Seminars in Teaching

The seminar as a form of academic activity undertaken independent of as well as part classroom teaching is placed between the lecture method and the workshop method, with respect to its level of formality. By seminars we usually understand an academic get-together in which well-prepared papers are read by one or more persons followed by discussions of a variety of kinds. The reading of papers is most fundamental to seminars. Seminars are not limited to the portals of schools and colleges; various organisations hold seminars as a usual practice.

A seminar is important because of a level of independence it has as an academic procedure to handle a topic of importance and to arrive at an understanding among the participants and to arrive at a set of conclusions. It does not have all the formality, seriousness, and pedantic nature of a lecture session and it is not far too practical and work-centred as the workshop is. A seminar offers opportunity for : 1. presentation of a short paper; 2. close contacts between the presenter and the audience; 3. inquisitive and searching questions on the part of the audience; 4. controlled and guided discussion on the topic covered; and 5. arriving at an understanding of a problem and its possible solutions on hand.

Seminars have been used as a regular procedure by all sorts of non-academic organisations because of these features that makes the procedure most feasible for an organisation to communicate to its members aspects of an area that they consider important. Guest speakers are invited to present papers on their areas of specialisation and the organisation enables its members to avail of these resources from time to time. While a lecture does not allow for considerable degree of discussion, a seminar is relevant because of its scope for intimate discussion. Discussion and listener participation are intrinsic to the very nature of a seminar and this characteristics gives the seminar greater scope for handling topics that are creative, communicative and perennial by nature.

Seminars thus have greater relevance to teaching. This method has been accepted as part of the college curriculum while its resource are not yet used by the school curriculum. There are a number of areas in the school curriculum where the application of the seminar method can be of greater benefit. The teacher both in colleges and schools can apply his mind on this academic procedure, identify components of the procedure that have immediate relevance to classroom teaching and thus make creative use of them.

6. Creative Aspects of the Seminar Method

Seminars have been conceived of in the present context as creative ways of enhancing academic work in schools and colleges in a manner that has traditionally not been thought of. The seminar method is a system which consists of a large variety of components or aspects that go into its making. The teacher should view the relevance of seminars from these aspects and try to tap its resources for the classroom.

1. *The Art of Presentation* : A seminar enables students to develop the art of presenting a discourse to an audience. Presentation of a paper or a talk to an educated audience is not a matter of joke. Lack of training in this aspect of academic life comes as an obstacle in one's professional life. It is not a training in public speaking which is a more scientific, enlightened and concentrated activity and requires training at a higher level. By presentation is meant here only those elements of public speaking that are required just for reading a paper in a meaningful and acceptable manner. A seminar is an opportunity for developing this specific element and the teacher, needs to keep this in mind while organising a seminar.

2. *Meaningful Interaction with the Audience* : A seminar helps students develop the ability to achieve meaningful interaction of an elementary kind with the audience. The reading of a paper puts the student in touch with an audience of a specific kind in the present case one's own friends or those of the same level. In order to read a paper in an effective manner one needs to learn a few technique among which meaningful contacts with the listeners is important. A paper is read aloud, and reading aloud is always meant for others. The teacher can workout the details of how these contacts should be maintained and take care of these while the student presents the paper.

3. *Developing the Paper* for the Seminar is an aspect that requires care and training. This is the stage when under the guidance of the teacher the student organises the material that will go into the seminar paper. The student will come to know how a topic is chosen, the preliminary points are developed, the preliminary writing is done and how through regular reference to source books and materials the final draft can be prepared. Each stage in the development of the paper needs care and training and will contribute to the academic skills of developing written or oral discourses with a research bend of mind. Seminars provide opportunity not only to develop and organise the paper like any ordinary material, but also do it keeping in mind the needs of the listeners and the role the discussion plays later.

4. *Reference and Gathering Information* : The seminar paper is supposed to be a scientific thing of a relative level, elementary or advanced. As such the material presented should have a theoretical basis for which the student should know how to use source books and materials. This is a form of reference and training is required to carry out reference in an effective manner. This skills is something for which students need to be trained at the school and university levels. The teacher should be in a position to guide the student in developing this skill of gathering materials from books. Seminars contribute to the development of the skill of reference in a significant manner. The nature of the work helps the student do reference at greater depth.

5. *Coordination of Materials and One's Frame of Mind* : Another important aspect of a seminar paper and its presentation is that it helps the student learn how to coordinate the information that he gathers with his frame of mind with reference to the topic. Even the student begins working on his understanding of a given topic unless some one writes the material for him and commits to memory. The student's understanding of the topic is the framework in which he will coordinate the new information or that forms the basic on which he will build the new information. The teacher can enlighten him in regards to the ways of doing this. This training is very fundamental to any serious research work or enquiry that the student will later take up. If this coordination is achieved the presentation of the paper at the seminar will be made most effective.

6. *Developing the Art of Collective Thinking* : Seminars provide opportunity to the students to engage in collective thinking. This is an aspect of the seminar. When the seminar paper is developed the student foresees the problems to some degree but collective thinking and group reasoning becomes a reality when the paper is presented. The student who presents the paper will not be in a position to impose his ideas on the group but is required to lead the group step by step in developing a discussion which means thinking and reasoning. The points of the matter are built in a given order and sequence in line with the framework he has projected on the paper. The group senses and comprehends this framework and joins the leader to workout the details of the discussion on the basis of the content of the paper.

7. *Answering Questions with a Focus :* Another aspect of the seminar is its potential to help students answer questions with a definite focus.

Since seminar is not just the presentation of the paper but is also leading a discussion and this aspect stands out clearly in the seminar. The framework of theory or practice that is presented through the paper enables the leader to answer the group's questions with a definite focus. This is true especially when the answer or reply requires some description. This description as it often happens can go astray or may have not much to do with the content of the question. Seminars provide practice in keeping a focus and work around this focus while answering someone's questions. The teacher needs to be aware of this aspect of the seminar and help the student while leading the discussion.

8. *Learning to Defend one's Points* : This aspects that seminar method projects has much to do with the metal training derived from this academic procedure. The seminar is an academic procedure that required the student to defend his ideas. He presents a body of information through the paper. This body of information will naturally have some or the other area that are relatively controversial. The student has made references and gathered information from certain sources and only he knows the nature of these sources and how valid his points are. On several such occasions he is expected to defend his ideas and view points during the discussion. This, again, requires training that is slow and painstaking. Seminars thus contribute to a major aspect of academic discussion how to defend one's viewpoint without hurting others.

9. *Learning to Revise One's Position* : Just as one needs to defend one's position that has a solid foundation, one also is required to revise and change one's position at a given instance when he know that others have provided arguments to the contrary. It often happens that a new insight is obtained or some one happens to highlight a point that we have not seen before, our standpoint has to be changed. It is called obstinacy when we keep on defending ourselves too far even after we are proved wrong. With a true sense of sportsmanship the student should learn how to give up his viewpoint and accept the new idea. Seminars help obtain opportunity to develop this habit and make the best out of it in organising a genuine discussion.

10. *Participant Involvement* : As in the case of tutorials, seminars too are the providing ground for student involvement and for generating high level interaction. Seminars organised in schools and colleges need to regard this aspect as very fertile. One or more students who read the

papers naturally obtain involvement; but on the basis of the several aspects of student participation the rest of the participants should be able to have involvement in the discussion and follow-up work. The teacher should regard this as an important aspect of the seminar and work towards the realisation of it in a most effective manner.

Every one of the aspects seen above goes into the making of what we have called a seminar. It is a system and as such an effective organisation of the system requires the realisation of these aspects and components as best as they could be. The teacher needs to be very conscious of this systematic perspective of seminar and guide students towards the effective implementation of these aspects.

7. How to Integrate Seminars into the Curriculum

Seminars are usually thought of as a mere decoration to the routine academic schedule of colleges and universities at the post-graduate level. The potential as a resourceful academic procedure has always been overlooked. As it has already been seen these academic activities are not mere decorations or part of the extra curricular schedule. The potential of these can be easily recognised from the detailed aspects and techniques we have examined. As such seminars in this particular case can be seen within the scope and purview of the regular curriculum and can be somehow or other knit into the very system.

Seminars should be planned out for the whole year in advance as part of the academic calender. The particular college or school should have a scheme for implementing the plan in such a way that it does not become a piece of decoration. The institution concerned will envisage the work from the academic benefits of the student body and overlook the possible inconvenience that the scheme may give rise to. First, the individual or the committee which looks after the work sits down and looks into the frequency of sessions that may be held within the purview of the regular schedule of the institution. A particular class can have a seminar once a week; this is the minimum one may think of taking into consideration and large number of students a class usually has at any level.

Second, the committee will look into the distribution of the seminar sessions at all levels so that it can arrive at a genuine coordination of the sessions at these levels without serious conflict. This coordination is required since the seminar sessions should need teachers as supervisors. Since a useful seminar can be had only with a relatively higher age-group, at the school level we may not think of lower levels for purposes of seminars. For purposes of convenience we may think it suitable only for the secondary stage where students have the necessary background of (a) language, (b) general information (c) subject information, and (d) exposure to books and magazines.

Third, the committee will take care of developing a pool of topics that is required for the seminars throughout the year. Unless this is taken care of, the programme as it is spread over the year will end up in confusion. The teacher or the committee chooses a large number of topics from areas related to the curriculum. This can be done in two ways : first, seminar topics may even be part of the subject matter that the syllabi cover; second, the topics may be co-curricular or from areas only somehow related to the subject matter of the syllabus.

Seminars can be integrated into the curriculum in two ways. It can be built into the regular classes. In this case it would be better to entrust this work to a language teacher preferably the teacher of English. It can also be done as part of the social studies classes in schools. Second, the whole thing can be done during extra hours, and an extra class can be allotted for the purpose. In this case the content of the seminar can be any one of the subjects at a given time and all the subjects can use this facility by turn.

The best thing to do is to build in the seminar as part of the regular classes. The teacher can use the seminar method as a classroom method. The following perspectives are important in this regard; if this scheme is followed no distinct arrangement becomes necessary. One period a week should be earmarked for this purpose. The schedule should be worked out in such a way that one subject will spare a period in a given week, another subject the following week and a third subject the third week. The burden would not thus fall on any one subject and the work can be evenly distributed. Std. IX for instance, would thus have a seminar period every week supervised by a particular subject teacher. The topic of the seminar will be from the subject whose class period is used for the purpose.

If the built-in scheme is followed again, both the class and the teacher will have considerable incentive for the work. A system which is not essentially part of another will have no one responsible. If the seminar is kept independent in schools, then this would be the result. The incentive comes from the fact that the seminar is part of the teacher's regular work and the work will prove beneficial to his subject.

The seminar method of teaching is regarded in the present context as an extra classroom dimension that has great potential for initiating in the classroom a degree of creative experience that is not part of the regular classroom methods. The various aspects and perspectives of the seminar method of teaching is analysed in detail so that the teacher should leave no stone unturned to find out vistas of information that are capable of enhancing his classroom teaching. The relevance and utility of this method are not limited to the language classroom. All the aspects we have considered in great detail are equally applicable to non-language classrooms as well. The first application of all these comes naturally to colleges and universities since the seminar method requires a certain minimum age-group to have the necessary academic maturity and background. But the present work envisaged the application of the seminar method also to school teaching because of its pervasive character.

4

WORKSHOPS
TECHNIQUES OF ORGANISATION

1. *Workshops as an Academic Method* : The regular classroom is the nucleus of all academic activities. The large variety of ways of working in the classroom makes the classroom unique in several ways. All the same the formal classroom is not the only arena for academic activities. Academic activities are carried out right from the most formal atmosphere of a *lecture hall* to the most informal, work-oriented and practical atmosphere of what has come to be called a *workshop*. A difference needs to be drawn among a large variety of ways of undertaking academic activities on a group basis, distributed between the two extremes of a lecture hall and a workshop. A *lecture* constitutes the most formal way of communicating to an audience a quantum of information in a manner that depends on the formality of the situation, ranging from a classroom to any other academic gathering.

Moving down the ladder one finds a *seminar* which combines the formality of a lecture and the work-characteristic of a simple discussion session. Seminars combine the formal presentation of material on a relevant subject matter combined with any form of discussions on the floor or in groups. A talk or the reading of a paper by one or more persons is very basic to any seminar. A *symposium* involves a number of participants who are expected to be well-acquainted with a field of knowledge. The participants give short talks on the topic under consideration in the form of a *panel* discussion. In this sense the two forms of academic activity have one and the same modus operandi, while a panel discussions can be a very simplified affairs undertaken even at the level of students.

The workshop method of carrying out an academic activity comes all the way down the ladder because of its unique characteristics. A workshop is down to earth, practical, work-based and task-oriented. The very label tells us that the object of the activity itself *is to get something done* rather than to communicate a quantum of information one way or other as in the case of activities mentioned earlier. The following can then be the *aims of a workshop* as we are envisaging it here : 1. A workshop aims at binding together people of identical interests or people with an identical purpose to exchange ideas, high light fields of study and to arrive at solutions to practical problems. 2. A workshop aims at providing the participants optimum opportunity to express their ideas and opinions and to actively participate in the decision-making. 3. A workshop aims at developing or enhancing a point of view, or aspects of a problem by offering the participants a *free atmosphere* and by collating information from the participants rather than provide them with a ready-made and pre-planned quantum of information. 4. A workshop often aims at purely practical things such as obtaining *materials* prepared or working out a scheme for any undertaking or further arriving at a practical outline of any project under consideration. Lastly, 5. a workshop can be evaluative by its very nature. It may be organised for the *evaluation* of any work done, materials prepared or scheme worked out.

Workshop method in other words, is an academic procedure for exchange of ideas or for getting a task done. Out of all the academic procedures we have examined workshop is the most down-to earth and task-centred. Participants feel free and at home because workshops provide the necessary atmosphere for exchange of ideas and expression of one's opinion. Because of its unique role as an academic procedure workshop method is used by organisations and agencies of all kinds to promote fundamental and specialised mode of communication. It has become the most scientific way for any agency to get any work done involving all its members.

2. Workshops and the School Classroom

Workshop method of academic work has not usually been thought of as relevant to the school classroom, or even of the college classroom. We have been trying to identify the workshop method with the group method of teaching. But this is not correct. Workshop method and group method have different potentials and should be used in the context of classroom teaching for different purposes. Just as group method has become a very basic classroom method which the teacher can confidently depend on for effective work, workshop method too has great potential as an academic method to be used in the classroom.

The term classroom is used not in its usual restricted sense in this context as a space-time organisational structure in which the teacher puts across a teaching unit or provides practice in a given skill. The term is used in the context of workshop method in a wider sense as will be clear from the following pages. Workshop teaching takes us out of the narrow bounds of the usual class room into an organisational structure similar to the academic activity that goes on in the outer world and provides an experience of a kind different from that of the regular classroom. As envisaged in the present context workshop method requires special arrangement other than the regular teaching hours. The following arrangement can be thought of for the purpose : 1. Two consecutive class hours be sandwiched out of the schedule and used for the workshop session. 2. Depending on the important and utility of the work an afternoon can be spirited out of the regular schedule and used for a full-fledged workshop session. 3. The last two class periods on a particular day of the week can be converted into workshop session. 4. at higher levels a day can be chosen from a few consecutive holidays and the students can be asked to spend a few hours for a useful workshop session on a very relevant topic.

Workshop sessions can take care of the following areas of teaching: 1. *Subject matter* that needs discussion and student participation but can not be handled in the regular classroom or as part of group method. 2. *Projects* that require decision-making and more elaborate work that can be adjusted within the scope of group method. 3. *Projects* that require unbroken and continuous work by way of planning, discussion or material preparation. 4. *Remedial programmes* that can be organised only at hours other than the regular class periods. 5. Activities that may not involve all the members of a class at the same time. These and other broad areas call for the utilisation of workshop method even in schools. The application of workshop method in the context of the school alters to a great extent the notion of the classroom as the only place where academic work can be done. The very notion of the classroom is altered in favour of more creative, purposeful and motivated work.

The following pages will show workshop method from a variety of view-points. These viewpoints are applicable to the school classroom and therefore need not receive focus here. There are numerous areas where the pupils require initiation and participation which at the same time cannot be handled within the scope of the forty-minutes class hour. By restricting teaching to and evaluating it only from such a classroom we are thereby depriving out pupils from a large variety of learning experiences that cannot be cut to size to suit our notion of the restricted classroom. Workshop method should assume the role of a regular curricular component and should be handled by the teacher not as a co-curricular or extra curricular component. The school should provide the teacher with the necessary elbow-room to exercise his mind on the application of such components to his regular teaching. All this would call for a little re-scheduling of the work, dropping a period for the better, combining a couple of class periods or inviting the pupils on a particular holiday for a bit of creative work that is well-planned.

3. Workshop Method and the College Classroom

It is the college classroom that is subject to the monotonous scheduling of the syllabus, and teaching becomes a matter of 'Syllabus presentation' with the word curriculum meaning nothing more than completing the items on the syllabus. It is true that the college classroom cannot become an arena of co-curricular activities because of the heavy premium we place on the content matter on the syllabus. The school syllabus offer guidelines for the materials to be used in the class, while the university syllabus directly offers guidelines for the work in the classroom. This heavy dependence on the syllabus makes university teaching pedantic, content-oriented and abstract and leaves the learner no room for diversion from the syllabus material.

Workshop method comes as help under such circumstances and the following could be thought of as the benefits that the college student can reap from workshop method. Workshops are seen essentially as a locale for maximum student interaction as in the case of group method. While the scope of group method is limited as part only of a regular class hour, workshop teaching can have scope for (a) longer duration of work, (b) bigger *space* than the small classroom, (c) greater *interaction* than would be initiative in one class hour, and (d) a *larger content* to be dealt with by the groups as compared to the usual group work.

These features make workshop method most suitable for college and university teaching. Workshops well organised will educate the students to enquire beyond the scope of the syllabus on which they have been trained to depend. They take part in regular classroom lectures as well as tutorials with group assignments and group work. But workshops that are schedules well introduce to them areas and vistas of knowledge that are both directly and indirectly related to the course. The student is exposed to experiences with a mode of enquiry and learning that are not part of the usual classroom. His thinking and critical sense are guided in directions that the student on his now in unable to do. In otherwords workshop teaching trains the college student's mind in the *spirit of enquiry* that is fundamental to any scholarship.

Workshop method of teaching educates the college student to examine things with an *analytic bent of mind*. Instead of all of a sudden coming face to face with the reality of *research* of a minor or major kind in one's advanced studies or professional life, the student learns through workshop method how to exercise his mind and critical sense in an analytic manner. The student requires fresh viewpoints, fresh opinions, details of a particular trend and material that will highlight a specific area in his field of study. Workshops provide opportunities for him to be exposed to these and equip with technique that will help him pursue the matter further.

Workshop method comes as a boon to students in cases of less gifted teachers for whom the syllabus frame itself is beyond their capacity. The classroom as a place where the learner derives a degree of intellectual satisfaction from the work done and information gathered, such teachers often leave a sour taste in the student's mouth. Workshops are envisaged in the present context as a partial solution to this problem since the teacher can create an environment where the students themselves make the enquiry, and acquire information on the topic under consideration. This is true of all subjects and all disciplines. If the teacher cannot provide adequate coverage of a syllabus he can find out ways and means in which the class will do the work for themselves in a large variety of ways. Workshop method is on among them. It is capable of helping the student enquire into the vistas of information that is ordinarily beyond his reach.

4. The Working Method of Workshops

Workshops have a characteristic mode of functioning. The very terms shows that something practical is intended and some amount of practical work is expected. Workshops can be described and distinguished from other similar academic activities in terms of the following characteristics.

1. A workshop is organised (a) to chalk out a decision, (b) to find solution to a problem, or (c) to develop a quantum of information for a particular purpose. In a workshop this is done not by one individual leader exposing his ideas and opinions and leading the group in a pre-mediated direction. A workshop is organised in such a way that the participants share a common back ground, common basis and are enlightened in the area more or less in the same degree. The participants of a lecture come to the lecture hall expecting to be well-informed about a particular topic that the speaker is expected to espouse. But the participants of a workshop come not with any such expectations, but hoping on the one hand to contribute to a, b, or c above, and the other to be indirectly enlightened by the discussion that is going on.

2. A workshop is not a strictly space-time bound academic activity as a lecture, seminar or group work in the classroom. A lecture or a seminar cannot be for that matter held in two or three separate rooms or it cannot be stretched indefinitely over a period of a couple of hours due to a number of constraints that are obvious. A workshop on the other hand can be conducted simultaneously in half-a-dozen rooms without in any way affecting its unified nature or in any way constraining the quality of work by the participants. A workshop may, similarly, be stretched over to a period of one or more weeks, not to speak of a day. This characteristic feature of workshop makes it useful for a large variety of purposes and its potential for the generation of work becomes considerably great.

3. The applications of workshops are great because of its unique modus operandi which he shall examine in detail on the following pages, This method permits the participants a very high level interaction and exchange in a single group or in smaller groups. Unlike a seminar there is no listening to any exposition or paper reading. The focus is not on any such initial expository work. In a lecture or seminar the expository work is important. In workshops the little introduction by the coordinator or any introductory exposition to a particular workshop session has a secondary role to play. Such a stress on the concrete discussion and work aspects of the workshop method enables it to create a most congenial

atmosphere for down-to-earth communication among the members of the group.

Because of the unique characteristics seen above, workshops play an important role not only in the academic sphere but also in other organisations and the resources of the workshop is tapped by these organisations. The question now is how to go about in the actual conducting of a workshop. The characteristics examined above are an indicator to the modus operandi of workshops. The following aspects are of help in the actual organisation of workshops.

1. *The Scheme of Work : Time Schedule :* A factor that fully controls the effect of any workshop is the nature of the scheme of work on which the workshop is based. This has several aspects. The first that needs consideration is the actual *Time Schedule*. The workshop has to be scheduled with care so that (a) the participants utilise every moment of the day, (b) optimum coordination of work can be obtained, and (c) the enthusiasm of the participants is properly maintained. A workshop may be conceived of for a duration of one week, for instance. Whatever needs to be done should be tightly scheduled into the one week. This one week is ear-marked for just one area, say for instance, *The Teaching of Grammar* (English). The workshop is held for teachers of English at the secondary level. It is undertaken as an *inservice programme* on the basis of their training as well as the teaching experience at the secondary level.

Time is allocated for the following aspects of the work : (a) introductory exposition, (b) workshop session (full group), (c) group discussion (smaller groups), (d) materials preparation, (e) demonstration sessions, (f) observation of relevant situations and materials on the audio-visual media, as well as (g) reference to source-books and materials. The time-table should be worked out in such a way as to given provision for all such relevant aspects that contribute to a productive workshop. Since the focus of the workshop is on the group work of all sorts maximum time on the schedule should be allotted to this, and introductory expositions should be done only on a very limited scale.

2. *The Scheme of Work : Content Division :*By content division we mean the proper distribution of the work load (in take and production) for the duration of the workshop. This requires some degree of expertise on the part of the organisers. We should be in a position to visualise the

content of work both holistically and analytically, i.e., as a system and as components of the system. The area, it sub-components, the skills involved, the quantum of information to be given for intake, the quantum of information that needs to be developed and organised as the end-product, the need of the participants to be exposed to theory, practice and materials etc., have to be thought of as part of the system. The organiser is required to have a holistic view of the whole system when he is scheduling its components for the functioning of the workshop. While dividing the area, for instance,. The Teaching of Grammer, for the workshop, efforts should be made to ensure maximum coverage of the aspects keeping well in mind the objectives of the workshop.

3. *The Scheme of Work : The Work Schedule* : The organiser needs to be aware of the role that the time-schedule, the content scheme as well as the work schedule play in the organisation of the workshop. If time schedule takes care of the time distribution with reference to the content distribution, the work schedule takes care of the practical output that is expected of the workshop. The content scheme delimits or expands the frame of reference in which the work needs to be done. The example that we referred to, "The Teaching of Grammer' gives the content scheme as the frame of reference in which the participants are expected to work concerетely in order to arrive at a regular scheme for the teaching of grammer at the secondary level. This will not mean developing new knowledge on grammer but organising usefully whatever knowledge is readily available on hand.

4. *The Size of the Workshop* : The group that will participated in a workshop has characteristic limitations. Its size is delimited by virtue of the kind of work that it is expected to go in. A lecture or a seminar for that matter can be attend by a very large number. It is not the same with a workshop. A workshop is like the group formed for group work, the major difference being the size. The function is one and the same. A workshop should ordinarily consist of less than forty participants, almost like a class. This is the maximum number one should think of any kind of a workshop. The most reasonable number should be thirty, while there should be a minimum of fifteen participant for a workshop to retain its character as a workshop. An eye on the size of the workshop group is in several ways important if one thinks of organising an effective workshop.

5. *The Formation of the Sub-groups* : Another aspect of the

organisation of the workshop is the formation of the sub-group. It becomes necessary to pre-arrange the workshop group into sub-groups for a number of reason. Small groups become necessary in order to work simultaneously on different content areas of the topic of the workshop as well as to produce materials with ease and compactness. Whatever decision-making, gathering of information, planning, or development of schemes or materials production that a small group of eight can do need not be taken up by the group of thirty. In other words it becomes necessary to differentiate the treatment of content matter between what is most proper to be done in the workshop session and what is proper to be done in groups. The number of sub-groups will depend on the sub-areas that needs to be worked on and the aspects of materials that should be produced. If the workshop ground is too small i.e. around fifteen, even a group of three could be yoked to workshop tasks.

6. *Presenting the Scheme to the Workshop Group :* It is advisable to place in the hands of the Group the Scheme of the entire work right in the beginning. This helps the Group in a number of ways. Access to the scheme and schedule of work helps the participants have an overall perspective of the work and thus have greater incentive to work through the sessions. Access to the scheme helps the participants get prepared in a number of ways as many would not like to cut a sad figure while working in the session or in grounds. Only a full perspective of the work will help the participants get sufficiently prepared.

7. *The Role of Hand Outs in the Workshop* : Handout materials have a major role to play in an effective workshop. A workshop is a tightly packed, task-oriented and supposed to be productive activity. The time is therefore most valuable. The introductory expositions, the content matter taken up for the perusal of the Group Session and the task of the groups etc., should be as far as possible placed at the hands of the participants. The best mode of doing this is through handouts. The handout could be just one sheet of paper at a time having the details or the outline worked out in a lucid manner. It helps greatly when at the end of the workshop the participants can carry home a whole bunch of such sheets filed neatly for his further perusal, orientation and study.

8. *Expository Talks* : All forms of workshops have place for what we may call expositor talks. The workshop sessions should begin every day with some kind of an introduction by a resource person who is a

participant of the workshop at the same time enlightened on the subject under consideration. The principal aim of this is just to initiate the workshop session as Group Session and not to teach the Group things that he may have in mind. In other words this introduction should never exceed ten minutes. In successive sessions this talk should naturally contain a recapitulation of the work done in the previous session as well as a prospective view of what should happen in the particular session. The material of the talk should be carefully chosen, organised and presented keeping in mind the very purpose of the workshop session.

9. *Demonstration* : Demonstration of some kind constitute part of most workshops depending on the need of the particular workshop. By demonstration we mean any kind of practical exposition meant to show the Group one or other aspect of the area under consideration that involves some kind of a practical skill. Since the workshop is organised at a place where resource persons and facilities are available, demonstrations of some kind can be arranged for the participants. Workshops of academic or non academic nature (industrial, organisational) can have demonstration of several kinds. Demonstrations may be in the form of *video presentation* or may be given directly resource persons. Since these demonstrations are strictly meant to highlight the practical dimensions of the workshop, these should be precise and up to the point and should not in any way be wasteful or disturb the schedule far too much. A single demonstration well done can save a great deal of discussion on the topic. All the same these should only be a help and never a substitute for the regular group work. The place demonstrations have in the teaching of languages is far too obvious to include here.

10. *Additional Experience in the Workshop* : The workshop schedule may include not only the components seen above but also several other components in the form of additional experience. I have here in mind mainly film, the television and the video. Exposure of the Group to particular and well selected films, video sessions and particular programmes on the television serves many things. It introduces variety in the Groups involvement through out the programmes. Such an exposure can also provide added expertise to the work of the Group. These function as additional experience for the Group and fill the gap in understanding the nature of the work and its complexities as part of the workshop.

11. *The Work of the Sub-groups* : What we have been calling "the Group' or `Workshop Session' consists of all the participants of the

workshop in full session. But the nature of the workshop is such that a major part of the decision-making, work in an area or materials preparation can be done in small groups that have been formed right from the beginning. The work of these groups is central to the workshop method. Right in the beginning a decision should be made regarding the difference areas where group work becomes necessary. As many areas of work there are, so many groups will be constituted. Thus the number of sub-groups depends on the different areas of work. The organisers should see to it that each group consist of people who can guide the work of the group, coordinate everything and present a satisfactory report.

12. *Preparation of Minutes* : Finally we should ensure that detailed minutes are prepared in the form of report to be used for follow-up work. Minutes are to be prepared of the introductory talks, Group Sessions, work of the sub-groups, demonstrations and all the components that have gone into the workshop. This work should be entrusted to someone who can do the work competently. This report will reflect the genuineness of the workshop, the nature of the organisation and the quality of the materials prepared as well as the work the participants have put in. The report of the workshop and the materials should reach the hands of the beneficiaries in time so that the advantages are reaped by them and everything can be open to constructive criticism and evaluation.

13. *The Role of a Check List* : Before the participants of the workshop depart we should ensure that an adequate check-list is turned in by them. The check-list that needs to be prepared in advance and should include all aspects of the workshop presented in the form of positive or negative statements. Its function is to evaluate whatever went on during the session and ensure a more effective organisation of the workshop on a following occasion, or at another venue. The check-list provides the participants an opportunity to express their opinion and grievances and call for a measure of reform in such workshops.

5. Workshops and the Teaching of Languages

The application of workshop teaching to the teaching of languages is great. Workshop method has several dimensions in this regard. As we have examined in Sec. 2 & 3, first, this method has applications to classroom teaching adding to the regular classroom extra-dimensions and thus extending the space-time bound classroom as well as the narrow syllabus to the dimensions that workshop teaching can offer. Second, workshop method is one unique method most useful for the following: 1. Preparation of syllabuses for language teaching; 2. Preparation of text-books and relevant materials for language teaching; 3. Developing area-wise strategies for teaching in rural-schools; 4. Developing strategies of teaching for urban schools; 5. Developing strategies and common schemes for evaluation in general and of examination in particular; 6. Developing scheme for the preparation of low-cost teaching aids for schools and for acquiring a right perspective in the use of such aids.

Again, (7) developing a perspective in the concrete use and application of technological devices for which the government has been investing sizeable amounts; 8. Inservice courses for language teachers at various levels; primary, secondary and higher secondary; 9. Inservice courses for teacher educators at various levels; Primary and Secondary; and 10. Workshops for coordinators of courses in centres of extension services where teachers can be offered relevant inservice courses. 11. Workshops for the preparation of software for the radio and the television.

In each of the above instances whose urgency is well recognised workshop method is of great service because of unique features. The list provided above includes three major areas: 1. Preparation of syllabuses, courses and materials for teaching languages; 2. Developing strategies that can guide methods, classroom techniques and evaluation in specific areas; and 9. Inservice courses for teachers and teacher educators at different levels. The resources of workshop method in these areas of language teaching has been very well recognised.

As seen in Sec. 3 above this method has relevance to college and university teaching. The following areas can be taken care of in the teaching of languages through workshop method. 1. Workshop can initiate students into comprehensive understanding and practice of the *skills of second and foreign languages* like English and French respectively. 2. Workshops can coordinate self-instructional sessions of a wider range than found in regular classes, to develop proficiency in particular areas of such languages. 3. Workshops are of help in providing college students training in the *academic skills* that they are desperately in need of. Workshop sessions can take care of the academic skills of (a) public spacing, (b) reading for reference purposes, (c) reference of dictionaries, source materials and documents, (d) note taking from reading, (e) note taking from talks and lectures, (f) oral presentation of discourses and (g) written presentation of materials with adequate, logical organisation.

Workshop method can also take care of work in the *content areas* in variety of ways. This method can train students to work independently and gather materials in the areas of the grammer and linguistics of a language, the history of a language, and of literature in its manifold perspectives. Workshop method comes as a help especially in areas where the restrictions and limitations of the usual class do not provide scope for more elaborate and detailed work.

6. Effective Communication in the Workshop

The workshop aims primarily at achieving optimum interaction and thus help participants make maximum contribution to the cause of the workshop. A workshop is not defined with reference to the quantum of learning that may take place, or with reference to the benefits that the individuals themselves derive from this activity. A high premium is placed on the output of the workshop in terms of the decision-making, organisation of information or materials production. In all the three goals of a workshop characterised as outputs, the participants are expected to (a) exercise their minds in a common direction, (b) shape their ideas and opinion to suit the common goal, (c) give expression these ideas and opinions in a way acceptable to others, (d) listen to what other participants have to say with a willingness to accept them, (e) understand others from their viewpoints and not from personal prejudices or with a biased mind, (f) respond to questions and points of discussion keeping in mind the common goal of the workshop.

Both the organisers and the participants have to keep in mind the need for *optimum communicative efficiency* in the workshop. There are a number of factors which contribute to this optimum communicative efficiency. 1. *The physical environment* in which the workshop is held contributes significantly to its communicative efficiency. The place at large, the situations of the room, the seating arrangement in the room, the lighting facility, room for work and movement, separate rooms for group sessions without interference and so on contribute to the level at which the participants can carry on with the discussion and the work.

2. *The language of liaison* is a major factor for successful communication in the workshop. If English is the accepted medium for

the work efforts should be made to use the same language constantly. In several cases the use of a language other than the regional language can cause a bit of hesitation and embarrassment; all the same it is greatly rewarding to make efforts to use a language that has for conspicuous reasons been chosen as the language of the medium. Individuals should make efforts to communicate using the common language inspite of their personal problems in the use of it. Efforts must be made to use a language for the workshop which has been the medium of scholarship in the field of study.

3. *The Expository talks* that have already been examined has much to do with successful communication in the workshop. The participants come to the workshop with a degree of uncertainty about the role they are expected to play. *The attitude of the speaker* who gives the expository talk influences the involvement of the participants and considerably influence their output. The speaker sets off a trend that may be monopolising or undemocratic by nature. The level of freedom which they feel is influenced by this trend that may continue upto the conclusion of the workshop. Hence those who introduce the work should do it in such a way as to set the correct trend that will create a most congenial atmosphere for the right sort of communication.

4. *Promoting Communication* : Apart from those aspects that promote effective communication, the organisers of the workshop may consciously resort to several other techniques for the purpose. Those who guide the Group Sessions should be constantly aware of the need for the greatest interaction and thus can manipulate the sessions to this effect. Handouts that are distributed from time to time helps communication in the Group affecting the very nature of the workshop proceedings. It is always courteous to ask for the opinions of those who usually remain silent. All these techniques can help promote communication in the workshop and make it most effective.

7. Materials Production in Workshops

An area where attention is needed is the production of materials in the workshop. In most cases some amount of materials will be produced as part of any workshop. But there are workshops held for the exclusive purpose of materials production. In the field of education, especially English language teaching, workshops can be venue for the production of a large variety of materials : 1. Syllabuses, 2. Textbooks, 3. Handbooks

4. Instructional materials for different levels, 5. Test materials for different levels, 6. Low-cost teaching aids for lower levels. 7. Software for language laboratories, 8. Software for the television, the view etc. 9. Software for radio presentations for teachers and students at various levels.

The application of workshop method for the production of materials in the areas mentioned above helps produce such materials with greater ease and efficiency as well as based on democratic principles. Materials production workshops need the following organisation. The organisers should be fully aware of the overall frame-work of the material that is going to be produced. The expository talks can present to the Group what exactly the purpose of the workshop is and present to him the broad frame work that has been thought out in advance.

The function of the Workshop Sessions is then to discuss things in detail, and arrive at the following perspectives : 1. The exact objectives of the materials under consideration; 2. Arriving at a consensus in regards to the broad framework of the materials as presented by the organisors; 3. Working out on paper the detailed sectionwise aspects of the material; 4. Developing the exact directions the material should take when the preparation will be in progress; 5. Allotment of sections to the sub-ground for perusal of the actual work; and 6. Actual working out of the sections of the material by the groups.

The groups constitute the avenue where the materials actually take shape. The following conditions are necessary for the groups to work most efficiently and for the full resources to be tapped. 1. The group should be sufficiently motivated for the work that needs care and thinking. 2. The group should have the right understanding of the exact work to be done. 3. The necessary physical amenities should be provided to the group for undertaking the work.

The groups should have access to reference materials to carry out the work satisfactorily. 5. The organisers and resource persons should be available from time to time to all the groups for consultations.

The materials take shape in the group. The members of the group carried out the preliminary correction and revision of the material keeping in mind the directions that the Group Sessions have set for the materials. The material is then presented to the Group for its criticism, evaluation and perusal. The best procedure for the Group then is to undertake a general discussion of the nature of the material after its presentation, and to pass the material on to another panel for an evaluative study and recommendations. This phase of the work is most valuable but care must be taken to see that such a thing should be done in a constructive manner keeping in mind the limitation under which the original group has worked out the material. This precaution is taken to ensure the quality of the material from the viewpoints of : 1. language, 2. content matter, 3. form of presentation, 4. instructional potentials and 5. organisation of the material. The sub-groups as well as the Workshop Session need to be aware of the problems that crop up in producing quality materials.

Workshop method and its potentials have considerable application to both academic and non-academic (organisational) spheres.

But the present work is interested in showing the relevance of this method as applicable to the academic sphere, education as a whole, the teaching of languages and in particular the teaching of English as second language. It is a creative dimension that leads the teacher as the regular classroom practitioner out of the narrow bounds of the classroom and helps him provide the sort of learning experience that the usual classroom cannot provide to the learner.

The biggest attraction of workshop method is its ability to initiate and maintain interaction at the highest level. What the teacher can do is to make efforts to tap the resources of this method for classroom teaching. On the basis of the outline offered in the present work the teacher should be in a position to work out the details as suitable to the teaching situations in which he finds himself. The scope of workshops needs to be fully understood by the teacher and the teacher educator so that as and when opportunities arise no one should hesitate to exercise one's mind in organising workshops within as well as outside the scope of the regular curriculum. The manifold effects of workshops of any kind will be most rewarding to the cause of the learning.

5

TEACHING THROUGH PROJECT METHOD

1. Essential Characteristics of a Project

Project method has been recognised in a academic circle as an academic procedure in which the potential of what we know as a project is utilised to provide the learner a variety of learning experiences. A project is an undertaking of any kind that has in it a scientific planning and a set of concrete directions with a heavy premium placed on its ultimate practical utility. A project in education would mean an undertaking with a practical bias which aims at *developing a system* in education with respect to educational theories or practices, or *producing in some kind of a material* on the basis of data framework that has been pre-conceived. A project has an *element of novelty* in it.

A project thus may consist of any undertaking right from the establishment of an educational institution or the writing of a book, down to a small-scale social activity in the neighbourhood or the preparation of a small write-up to be put up on the school bulletin board. Any project, therefore, is something well-planned, has a definite direction as an undertaking, has a practical dimension as a concrete activity, and emerges as a system. The following characteristics are central to a project as a concre to undertaking:-

1. *Creative Imagination*: A project is built on creative imagination. It is an undertaking in the form of developing a system where the individual on the one hand applies and on the other develops his creative imagination. It is called a project for this very purpose. The whole

undertaking begins on the foundations of creative and imaginative planning. It is creative because as an undertaking it does not consist in repeating or reproducing what already exists as a system. If this happens to be so then we do not label it a project. It is creative because the individual exercises his mind top achieve a reorganisation of elements that may exist in some form. The creative dimension comers from this reorganisation. A project is essentially imaginative because the end-product is pre-conceived in terms of a set of mental images that do not as such exist outside. The individual builds and gives shape to this end-product in his mind and an imaginative construct. Thus by the time the project takes shape he will be reconstructing this mental construct as a reality based on his creative imagination.

2. *Novelty as Basic*: The element of novelty is fundamental to any project. A project is creative and imaginative and requires the individual to exercise his mind in novel directions. However simple or complex the project may be the element of novelty makes it characteristic. By novelty is meant that dimension of the project which is unique to it and differentiates it from other undertakings. There can be novel features even in a simple write-up and these novel features make a simple write-up attractive. The novel features may consist in the combination of already available elements or in a degree of addition made to an existing element. A simple picture cut out from a magazine will be converted into a project for the wall-paper when the student combines that cut-out with a small poem borrowed from another source. The combination makes it novel. It can also be that the student composes a few lines, or draws a picture for an original poem, in either ways he has used his creative imagination to give birth to a project.

3. *Coordination of Skills*: A project has an inherent potential to help the individual to combine and coordinate a number of skills. In fact every project is a combination of a variety of skills that the individual exercises. The following skills may be considered basic to a project: 1. the spirit of enquiry, 2. discourse development, 3. painting and drawing, 4. planning out sub-elements, 5. organisation of ideas, 6. aesthetic judgement, 7. a sense of proportion and beauty, 8. ability to judge maximum relevance etc.. A project combines these and other skills and helps the student achieve a harmonious coordination of several intellectual, sensory and manipulatory abilities that usually go into the production of projects.

4. *Visual Expression*: A project as understood in the present context has the visual component (modality, stimulus) as a central element. We do not think of a project of a purely aural-oral structure in which only the additional modality is at work. A project is conceived of as something written, drawn, a combination of both, something made or worked out. In all such cases the central mode of expression is the visual element. Visual expression is therefore central to a project. The level or the degree at which this modality functions depends on the kind and complexity of the project. The individual thereby undergoes an experience of manipulating visual components (poems, pictures, things, write-ups) in variety of ways.

5.*Coordination of Multiple Stimuli*: The effectiveness of learning depends very much on the coordination of the variety of stimuli presented to the learner. Projects by their very nature do have a variety of stimuli going into their making. The learner is given opportunities to manipulate such stimuli and work with a definite sense of direction. A project has scope for introducing verbal and non-verbal stimuli. In non-verbal stimuli the learner manipulates drawings, sketches, pictures, and other two-dimensional aspects as well as a variety of objects and models. A project helps the learner handle all these not merely as random play things but with an aim and direction, with a view to producing a creative, imaginative system. The student learns to harmonise these multiple stimuli into a total effect as pre-conceived by him. This is a major training that projects are capable of giving.

6. *A Research Bent of Mind*: This is one of the major contributions of a project, and thus goes into the making of a project. Research is a big term that can also be used for a minor thing such as a rudimentary project. Research is an investigation or an enquiry carried out in a scientific way to solve a problem or produce a system i.e., a theory or practice. It is an attitude or a bent of mind that needs to be developed right from the beginning of an individual's education. A simple project contributes to this training in a significant way. It sets in the student an urge to search for meanings, aspects and solutions. It helps him work with a definite direction, coordinate experiences, harmonise sense stimuli and work for a definite goal. It helps him search for relevant information and materials that should go into the work and coordinate or organise the information and materials to a total effect. By a research but bent of mind we mean exactly this.

7. *Learning Through Enquiry* : Most classroom experiences come to the learner in the form of spoon-feeding. Students, especially the bright learner group is simply snubbed due to the lack of challenging work. A project as seen above helps the student learn not from stereotyped textbooks or materials, but by going out of the limits of classroom work, gathering materials, Research as seen above is product-oriented while enquiry as we think of it here is a learning technique. The teacher only creates the right atmosphere or directs the student to such an atmosphere in which correct and effective learning will take place. This is a component of a project.

8. *Organises Thinking and Imagination*: A project helps the student not only develop manipulatory skills and coordinate sense experiences but also organise thinking and imagination. Thinking has ideas and its content while imagination works on images as the raw-material. The student in course of his education undergoes learning experiences which help him coordinate the two: ideas and images, thinking and imagination. The traditional classroom with purely verbal stimuli employed for teaching seldom provides opportunity for the development of these. Project work makes the student think independently and develop his ideas on the one hand, and on the other use his imagination in a creative manner, introduce and develop new perspectives, and thus produce effects that the traditional classroom cannot produce.

9. *Principle of Do and Learn* : A project, again, has another relevant component that makes it different from most traditional ways of learning. A project realises the principle of do and learn. No project is a mere abstract organisation of ideas without involving some manipulatory skills. It involves some degree of doing of one kind or other. The student is given opportunities not merely to see others doing things but to do things himself. This develops in him an unparalleled confidence. Doing here does not mean any random classroom activity as what the teacher might initiate while teaching a grammer item. Doing here is an organised thing, more complex and has an independent aim on hand that the usual classroom activities do not have.

10. *Achievement Motivation* : A project is a system that has rare potential to increase the student's achievement motivation. The student either takes initiative to do a project on his own or the teacher assigns him a project. In either ways he is doing something that the rest of the class do not do at a given time. This unique opportunity arouses in him

a great sense of motivation, and helps him recognise his own aptitudes in doing things. Achievement motivation is a circular thing : the more and opportunities to do things the greater the achievement motivation and vice-versa. Projects are systems that can easily set in motion in the student this circular experience. The teacher in the classroom has techniques to enhance this component of learning but projects do it in a unique manner and thereby helps the student to project this motivation to other areas of his academic performance.

2. Project Method : General Projects

Project method is seen in a present context as the application of the principles, aspects and potential of projects to classroom teaching. The components of a project as seen in detail in the preceding section are aspects that the teaching is expected to focus on. An awareness of these components helps the teacher work with a definite sense of direction. The teacher conceives of the project method of teaching not as an extra-curricular activity alienated from regular class work but as inherent to the class work. A project is never assigned to be done as part of the regular teaching work in the class, but all projects emanate in the classroom can be bound with the classwork and will benefit the student in doing his regular study with greater efficiency. The following can be the scope of the project method of teaching with respect to its classification and characteristics. All projects in the present context as classified under two major heads : 1. *General Projects*, and 2. *Language Projects*. General projects are thought of here as relevant to and inclusive of all subject areas including language teaching. Language projects are specifically geared to the needs of second language teaching and worked out with reference to the skills and components of language, with particular reference to English. The following are the categories of projects that may be considered general projects:

1. *Newspapers and Magazines* : Projects can emanate out of news-paper and magazine clippings. There are two ways of doing this. First, the teacher can allot topics relevant to his subject and ask students to gather material from newspapers and magazines for the particular project. Second, students can be trained to be on the look out for materials from newspapers and magazines, and the work should be left to topics of their choice. In either case the planning for projects based on newspaper and magazine clippings should begin from the teacher. It has to be

organised in such a way that the work can be done on a voluntary basis or students for the purpose can be chosen by the teacher himself.

The project may be for instance on *Wild Life in India*. The students responsible for the work are guided about gathering pictures of animals and aspects of wild life that are available from magazines. The nature of the project as a creative work will be retained only if things are gathered from different sources and are organised by the student in an original way. It doesn't become a project if he lifts an article on 'Wild Life' from a magazine and puts it up on the bulletin board. He should choose pictures and provide the write-up, or he should choose the write-up and provide the necessary pictures from other sources. The student should be able to use his imagination to organise and give a final touch to the project. Once the project is finalised it has to be exhibited for pursual and study by others. Newspapers and magazines provide great scope for very creative and useful projects.

2. *Experiments at Home* : Projects based on small scale experiments at home provide scope for work especially in science subjects. The experiment would mainly be in understanding the physical, chemical and biological laws and functions of Nature. Students can easily be enthused to undertake rudimentary home-experiments. The actual experimentation is only the basis of the project. The student plans the experiment, works it out in line with the teacher's guidance and aims at preparing a report of the actual work done. The report is the core of the project as it is meant for others to followup. The student plans out the form of the report with the teacher's help, gathers pictures if available, draws diagrams and sketches if necessary and coordinates these elements of the project. He writes a report of the actual work done depending on the scope of the work, organises the write-ups and illustrations, and presents the whole thing as a project. The project is put up in the school in the individual's or the group's name.

3. *Observation of Nature* : The project method of teaching can in several ways help students observe Nature. Students should be taught how to undertake scientific observation of aspects of Nature around us. The teacher should exercise his mind to develop a pool of areas related to Nature study. This pool will consist of topics that range from geography to biology. Students will choose from these topics areas that they prefer to work on. These need not involve travelling to distant places. Instead aspects of Nature as found around one's home : trees and plants, animals

and their habitat; birds and their habitat, fields and plantations, forests and river-beds, flower gardens and parks and all aspects of life around us can be the object of the observation of Nature. The student should have a framework to study a given aspect of Nature. This he develops in consultation with the teacher. The project takes the form of a write-up in which if possible he makes use of pictures. Once the project is finished the material is put up as a project on the observation of Nature.

4. *Sports and Games* : Just as Nature is made the object of study under the project method, sports and games can be taken up as the object of such study. The student who is assigned such an area is guided as to what aspects of a game to observe. This can especially be done when important competitions take place around the area. The student knows what to look for and how to describe it later. While observing a game he keeps in mind those aspects he has been asked to observe.

The project will consist of a description of the various aspects of the game in short or in detail depending on the scope of the particular project. The student finds out a set of related pictures or can draw pictures for that purpose and organises the write-up and the pictures. These projects are useful especially for those students who do not know the various aspects of that game or how that game was played at that particular instance. Projects of this kind exposes to students aspects of daily life and experience to which every one may not have access.

5. *Projects on Reading* : It need not be stressed that reading constitutes the best background for the development of projects. Every student at all levels is exposed to some degree of reading other than the classroom material. It may be short stories, children's books, descriptive accounts from magazines, materials from newspapers, novels, poems, and books on national heritage. Students individuals cannot afford to neglect some degree of reading from early days. The teacher should have plans to tap this source to develop materials for projects. Different students are exposed to different kinds of material and project method will bring all these right into the classroom. The teacher should have a project framework and a scheme to draw materials from various sources which children are exposed to. Projects can be worked out as summary material, short description, short narration, dialogues, short stories, picture description and so on. These write-ups are based not on direct experience as observation but on reading. The creative part of the work consists in drawing material from these sources and presenting in the

project as re-organised material. A long story shortened into a presentable from requires creative skill on the part of the student.

6. *Television and Video Projects* : At a time when students are exposed to the television and the video, the teacher should have very creative ways of tapping such a resource for the classroom through the project method. There are numerous educational and semi-educational programmes on the television and such material children come across on video presentations. The teacher can workout a frame-work in which such programmes, presentations and materials can be worked out into projects. Once students know that fine projects can be produced out of T.V. and video presentations; they will be on the look out for such programmes. It requires only the right understanding of how to convert a programme into a project and this has to be provided by the teacher. The material thus prepared has to be worked out in a presentable form if possible with illustrations wherever it can be done and is brought to the class for others to read and pursue.

7. *Specimens and Models* : Projects can be based not only on magazines, newspapers and story books, but also on three dimensional objects such as specimens and models. A project as a creative undertaking can use shells, coins, stones, flowers, leaves, insects and any-thing that the students can lay hands on. Projects can also be based on a large variety of models such as those of vehicles, buildings, machines, electric gadgets and so on. It becomes a project when a specimen is made use of or a model is constructed by the student as part of the work and presented to the class or school of wood. Specimens and models are projects have greater relevance in some subjects than others. Depending on the need of the particular subject more or less importance can be attached this particular kind of projects.

3. Language-Specific Projects

Projects that are examined on the preceding pages are general projects which can be part of any subject at the school level. The work in such cases is not attached to any very specific area unless specified by the teacher while recommending topics for a particular subject. Language specific projects are by their very nature attached to the various skills and components of a language. The following projects may be considered most useful as part of especially in the learning of a second language like English. In all these cases the project aims at the development and practice of that aspect of the language for which the project is designed.

1. *Grammer Projects* : Projects can be designed in the areas of the grammer of English. In this case the student is allotted a topic in the functional grammer of English such as, say, any of the tenses. Since English grammar has scope for a great variety of project topics, each student can be allotted topics for projects in the area of grammer. The project can be prepared as cursive write-ups, list of sentences using the tenses, exercises using objective items, a short discourse in which the tense is used and so on. As a project it is most recommended to use illustrative pictures or sketches. The student should aim at the right coordination of the language material with the pictures. Again, as far as possible the language should be prepared by the student himself and corrected by any one else.

2. *Projects on Pronunciation* : The Pronunciation of English can be the material for projects. Pronunciation includes : consonants, vowels, depthongs; patterns of stress, pitch, tonal contours; and aspects of conversational English such as ways of greeting, modes of address, patterns of questions as well as several colloquial aspects of English. The teacher of English will distribute such aspects of pronunciation and conversational English in such a way that there will be adequate coverage of these areas in the preparation of projects. The student who is assigned a project on the vowel system of English, for instance will prepare a chart on which will be presented representative words that carry the English vowels. At this level the phonetic symbols may not be taught or used. All work can be done by the use of word-groups which carry the typical English sounds as well as sentences and expressions that carry stress and intonation. The conversational aspects of English can be represented by the use of dialogues that are prepared well. Such projects are of great use to others in the learning of English.

3. *Projects on Vocabulary* : The vocabulary of English can become effective material in the preparation of projects. The objective in this case is to acquaint students with the expression as well as recognition vocabulary of English at the school level. The teacher makes a list of what may be called registers or topics on which the students can work. Each student will be given a particular register. The student who, say for instance, works on the register 'garden' on his own tries to develop a set of vocabulary items related to 'garden', organises the vocabulary in a

particular direction, and presents the set on a project paper. The teacher of English will make use of such a project not only for students' use in general but also for his regular classroom work in the form of instructional materials. Projects on vocabulary can also include: idioms, phrasal verbs, synonyms, antonyms, cries of animals, young ones of animals, habitats of animals and a large variety of aspects that will be of great use to enrich students' vocabulary.

4. *Projects on Reading* : Projects on reading in English aim at a number of things : increase in reading speed, increase in reading comprehension, proficiency in expression vocabulary and recognition vocabulary, and proficient in discourse development. Reading in English aims at all these aspects of the English language and reading contributes to all these aspects of the English language and reading contributes to all these in several ways. Students should be trained in preparing projects based on their reading. The teacher should in this case ensure that the student have books to read either provided by parents at home or by the teacher himself from the school library.

The material of students reading becomes the material for the project. The reading for the purpose can be done in the class as an extensive reading session or as supervised library reading. The project may be based on any narrative or descriptive material to which the student is exposed. While reading he should be conscious that a project will be prepared out of the material. The project can be done either in a discourse from (Sec. 2:5) or can be on the vocabulary from the reading material. The student should undertake the organisation and presentation of the material on project paper. The material thus put up can lead others to the source as well as they will benefit from the discourse or list of vocabulary put up as the project.

5. *Write up Projects* : All projects in some form or other get finalised as write-ups. But the source of all such projects are material that the student comes across elsewhere. In write-up projects as conceived of in the present context, the student does not depend on any material from outside. He works on it in the form of a composition or discourse construction. The basis of such a project can be the regular composition that the teacher works on in the class. The teacher develops on oral composition without a picture or a picture composition using a picture. The material thus developed through questioning is used by the students

for discourse construction (oral). In otherwords the student who is going to undertake a write-up project has all the background in a composition class. The teacher can distribute his regular composition to one or two students at one time to be worked out as projects. The student uses the points developed in the class and one or more pictures and finalise the project for display in the class or at the school.

6. *Projects on Poetry* : English poetry offers considerable scope at the school level for useful projects. This is true especially when the textbook at a particular level does not have a fair number of poems for study. In such cases projects can be used as a means to introduce poems from outside the textbook. The teacher can show the students sources from where poems are available, such as poetry books in the school library or at home. Once a poem is selected the student should be able to find a couple of pictures to go with the poem or get a picture drawn for the purpose. If the poem is small the student at a higher level can prepare a write-up of a few lines to go with it. The project then can be displayed for others to read and enjoy as well as use it for other purposes like recitation.

There are numerous areas in which language projects of a very creative kind can be prepared by students. In addition to those mentioned above the following can be considered useful as projects. For English : 1. *Exercise projects* based on grammatical exercises in English using objective test techniques for pursual by students. 2. *Graphics projects* based on the orthographic system of English to acquaint students with the details and problems areas of English graphics. 3. *Spellings projects* based on the spelling rules and exceptions as well as spelling groups that represents the various sounds in English language. 4. *Process projects* based on the tenses and other areas of grammer than indicate processes of various kinds found in our day-to-day lives. Pictures play a major role in such process projects. All these are language specific projects geared especially to the needs of second language learning.

4. Project Method as Curricular Activity

Project method of teaching is usually seen as something unrelated to classroom teaching and as such not part of the curriculum. We have already seen how projects are essentially curricular and this resources can be tapped for regular classroom teaching. The present work conceives of projects at two different levels ; curricular and co-curricular which also includes extra-curricular dimensions of projects. The teacher needs to be fully aware of the curricular dimensions of project method. Projects are systems that can bring into the classroom aspects and dimensions of life that the textbook or other instructional materials do not. A project can emenate from the classroom or from at home depending on the role the teacher plays in the origin of a project. Whatever be the original conception the material that goes into the project belongs to sources outside the classroom. By means of the project these materials are selected, coordinated and organised, and are presented to the class for its study and pursual. In otherwords projects do the function of bringing into the classroom aspects and dimensions of experiences that are not ordinarily available to the classroom.

A project becomes curricular when the content of the project has direct relevance to the textbook or aspects of teaching that goes on in the class. The teacher will employ project method to directly enhance classroom teaching when the chooses areas that are part of his work in the class. The language specific projects examined in the preceding section can all be curricular by nature. In these cases the teacher is using project method to go with his classroom teaching. This can be true of language teaching or teaching of other subjects where content specific projects are prepared.

The teacher of English while engaged in the teaching of a particular subject of 'Reported Speech' in English can very well assign to a couple of students one or two projects to be prepared are reported speech. The projects will be based only one or the other area of the grammatical structure. The students concerned will develop the material in the form of a dialogue according to the teacher's instructions, a write it down on project paper. This material will be displayed in the class for all the students to read and study the use of the structures. Materials of this sort will help the class to take note of that particular aspect of English language from a fresh perspective because a project is not ordinarily part of classroom teaching. Even if no extraordinary material is used, the very presence of the project in the class or school bulletin board will ensure students' attention on the particular aspect that is part of the course.

The scheme for project work should be integrated into the school curriculum as discussed in the preceding sections. This integration calls for the choice of topics only from the subject matter taught at the school. By integration we mean the right coordination of classroom teaching and the textbook with the areas taken up for project work. The teacher should feel responsible for providing the right guidance in this direction. When projects directly contribute to a particular course on the curriculum then the projects become curricular by nature. The teacher will envisage the right integrity of classroom techniques, teaching materials and the projects. Projects will then function like the 'eyes' of the classroom. Through the projects can will be able to see the quality of the work going are in the class. All projects are prepared at home unless special provision is made for projects at school. But the work commences in the classroom and the product is put up in the classroom for every one's pursual. As such project work retains the quality of being curricular. Again, the curricular nature of projects also depend on the teacher's involvement in the preparation of these.

5. Project Method as Co-curricular Activity

Co-curricular aspects of the curriculum consist in those activities of the school and college which are not strictly part of the mainstream of work such as the syllabi and the course work, but in one way or other *contribute* to the development of the curriculum. Co-curricular aspects are thus related to the curriculum and are definable with reference to the curriculum. Extra-curricular activities on the other hand are not directly definable with reference to the curriculum, but fulfil broad educational objectives in a rather remote manner. Classroom teaching is curricular, for instance, an elocution competition held in the school is co-curricular while a programme of cleaning a road in the near-by village as a community activity is what I consider extra-curricular by nature.

The project method of teaching has been seen in its curricular dimension. Project method has also a co-curricular and perhaps extra-curricular dimension. When the project begins from and ultimately contributes to a course of study it becomes a curricular activity; where a project is only somehow related in content or skill to a course, in particular to a subject, it becomes co-curricular When a project makes only a remote contribution to a course of study we shall consider it extra-curricular. Numerous projects can be assigned to students on such areas that are only related to a language or a subject. When students are in the habit of preparing projects initially with the guidance of a teacher and then on their own initiative, they come out with projects which do not strictly form part of a specific course. A project prepared from a television programme on the migration of birds shall not be considered curricular with reference to the learning of English. But such a project is done in English and therefore contributes directly to the study of English. We shall call this a project with co-curricular dimension.

Projects of co-curricular dimension has several advantages too. Co-curricular projects are capable of introducing a lot more of variety in learning because of the scope these projects have for enthusiastic students. Curricular project need strict direction from the teacher and they are restricted to the scope of the work done in class or to the scope of the instructional material used by the teacher including the textbook. Co-curricular projects on the other hand can be of any area or topic so long as they are somehow related to or can make contributions to the actual work in the class. The scope of these projects can enthuse the bright learner group of the class since these students are always in need of challenging and extra work to keep themselves occupied. The teacher can easily yoke these students to project preparation.

6. Skills Involved in Project Method

Project method is conceived of in the present context as a system itself. As a system it consists of aspects, components and perspectives that are inherent to and are intrinsically bound with the system. We have so far seen in detail what these aspects, components and various perspectives of the system of project method are. As a system thus project method becomes effective because of a large number of skills (see 1 :3) that go into its making. These skills constitute part of the aspects of project method but are distinguished from other aspects because of the unique characteristics of these skills as means to the development of the individuals's aptitudes i.e. ability to handle things and situations.

1. *Ability to Organise Enquiry* : Development of the individual's ability to organise enquiry into a given phenomenon is very central to project method. Projects can contribute significantly to the development of this skills. A project by its very nature is a novel and creative thing. It is not a replication of anything else readily available. The student is required to search for the component material that will constitute the project depending on the level at which he works, look for perspectives in the development of the project, and obtain directions to its finalisation.

All these call for a level of intellectual enquiry and physical search for relevant materials. This develops in him a skill that is most fundamental to education. This skills is a part of the system we have called projects.

2. *Developing a Scheme* : However rudimentary a project may be it calls for a certain degree of schematisation in the form of organising a few ideas, using a couple of pictures and so on. A good project has a considerable degree of schematisation going into its structure. Developing a scheme or schematisation is thus a skill that is inherent to a project. By developing a project the student is thereby developing the skill of schemeatisation. The topic selected for the project is worked out into sub-topics and further into sub-divisions until the last runs of the ladder is arrived at. It is again a fundamental skill necessary for later academic activities.

3. *Organising Ideas* : A project involves the skill of organising ideas with a focus on the topic. While schematisation deals with the planning chiefly of the formal aspects, organisation of ideas takes care of the content matter. A project helps develop this skill that goes into all sorts of academic activities including all forms of teaching. The project is centred on a topic and the student has to organise ideas under each sub-topic and sub-division. The presentation of the material becomes effective depending on the degree of organisation that has gone into the material.

4. *Aesthetic Judgement* : A project by its very nature involves the skill of aesthetic judgement. A project is defined as a creative undertaking with an imaginative core in it. The student has a given degree of aesthetic judgement at a given time. Aesthetic judgement is the ability of the individual to evaluate the degree of beauty that either a thing reveals or a thing requires. A project as a creative undertaking has inherent in it certain degree of beauty and proportion. The aesthetic level that a project can be raised to depends on the judgement of the student at a given time. Preparation of projects in a variety of ways help the development of this skill.

5. *Ability to Judge Relevance* : A project develops in the individual an ability to judge relevance at a given instance. The preparation of a project means value judgement at different levels. The student will be exposed to written materials, ideas pictures and objects of a variety of kinds pertinent to the project. He is required to undertake a value judgement at different stages as to the adequacy of the material he is

choosing for the project and as to the adequacy of a given material at a given place. This ability to pass value judgement is a major skill involved in project work. The student who prepares a project has thus opportunities to develop this skill in several ways.

Apart from the skills mentioned above a project is characterised by other skills : painting and drawing, coordination of multi-sensory elements, coordination of aspects in a discourse, discourse development and a variety of other skills depending on the level at which one works. Taken seriously and working with a definite sense of direction projects prove to be of great value in developing several intellectual and manipulatory skills.

7. How to Work on Projects

Lastly, we need to consider how exactly to go about in the preparation of projects. Project takes a student through several distinct stages before he is in a position to display it on the class or school bulletin board. The work begins when the student selects a suitable topic for the project either with the help of the teacher or the parents. Mostly this can happen if any cue for a project is available from any source. Once the topic or the area is chosen, the student enters the planning stage. Here the student is expected to workout the direction of the projects, the sub-topics, the main content, the kind of illustrations to be used and so on. The plan has been explained above as schematisation. As he begins gathering materials including picture the scheme or the plan will be revised and new aspects will be added.

Then begins the stage of materials collection. The success of a project depend considerably on this stage when the student will be on the look out for materials. To develop the write-up according to the scheme the student needs to look through newspapers, magazines and periodicals that are available in the schools, at home and in the neighbourhood. He is on the look out for any writing on the topic that he may use for the purpose. Along with the write-up he is on the look out for pictures that can go with the write-up in the project. The sources mentioned above are looked up for pictures too.

After gathering the available material the student sits down to patch the pieces together, to coordinate the material itself and to coordinate the write-up with the pictures. This is a stage further than the selection and decision making. The final part of the work consists in preparing the write-up and the pictures on projects paper according to the guiding teacher's suggestion. Then the project is displayed on the bulletin board either of the classroom or of the school, for the rest of the school to follow-up. The project method is an asset to the academic character of the school and if taken seriously will contribute to the academic development of the student in a very significant manner.

6

COMMUNICATIVE STRATEGIES FOR THE CLASSROOM

1. Communicative Dimensions of Teaching

The term 'communication' has so numerous connotations that it is futile to define it with reference to any one of these connotations. Communication engineering, psychology, linguistics and a number of other fields of study have many things to say about communication. Communication means in general an exchange of a vocal nature between two agents expressing an idea or an intention Under this notion we are able to speak of (a) animal communication and (b) human communication. Human communication can be (a) non verbal and (b) verbal. Non-verbal communication includes all forms of sign communication that man is capable of doing including gestures and social expressions. Verbal communication includes (a) verbal symbolic and (b) verbal non-symbolic communication. Verbal non-symbolic communication includes all forms of vocal expression and sounds that man is capable of producing, that have only a sign value, for instance a cought communicating to X the presence of Y.

What we call language proper is, in short, *verbal Symbolic communication*, Language alone has a symbolic value deeper, differentiating and with greater variables than a mere sign has. Language with its symbolic value can be compared to the National flag that represents a big range of value system, while a sign can be compared only to the red flag in the hands of a railway guard, which has only a sign value: danger, stop! It is this symbolic value that enables the words and combinations of words in a language to have different levels of meanings or connotations, and constitutes what is called the 'sematic system' of language.

Language with the elaborate symbolic values has a number of functions to do. The most basic, and all pervasive of such functions is *communication.* Another important function of language is aesthetic expression. Language and communication have come to be regarded as more or less synonymous because aspects of communication other than language in society are most insignificant as compared to what language does in society. Language must have for all reasons originated in human society as a means of communication as developed from most primitive modes of communication. All other functions that we may conceive of with reference to language have been realised only later in the history of man, such as the use of language for man's creative, aesthetic expression.

Language, therefore, has forms grammatical and functions and meanings which cater to note only the communicative needs of man but also for other purposes. Compared to the narrow definition of communication that we have assigned to language, we can see that man is able not only to express himself but also to hide his thoughts and feelings in the use of language, to use language to provide a double meaning in a given situation and so on. In other words human language have been developed to such an extent that they contain hosts and forms, functions and meanings that are outside the scope of pure communication purposes.

A second language such as English in India can be understood with reference to its primary role only from this perspective. This communicative function of language has come to be called *communicative competence*. Communicative competence is the built-in language ability of the individual that makes him capable of communicating himself effectively to others using that been called *communicative strategies.* Language consists not only the structural components such as sounds, grammer and lexis but also a set of strategies or devices that help the speaker carry out interpersonal communication with optimum efficiency in a given *communicative context*. Language does not take place in a vacuum. It is produced in all its concreteness as an event, what we shall call the *communicative act*. All communicative events (acts) take place in given communicative contexts which are in fact social contexts of one kind or other.

While setting our goals for teaching English in India we have to keep in mind these perspectives of the *communicative dimensions* of language in general and English in particular. Although all aspects of English as a language are in one way or other important to the learner in the classroom, the learner as some one prepared by the classroom as a speaker of English for the community, these communicative dimensions of English langauge need precedence over all others. The learner should be exposed to that kind of English which helps create a communicative event or function satisfactorily in such an event. The learner should be exposed to that English which is communicative and not textbookish. The learner should have at his disposal aspects of English language that will help him carry out the functions of daily life. The learner, again, should be exposed to that knowledge of English which help him choose at a given instance linguistic options (words, expressions) that convey his information and intentions with consideration economy and ease. All these aspects are central to the communicative dimensions as relevant to classroom teaching.

2. Communicative Dimensions of L_1 Classroom

The L_1 (first language) speaker as a learner comes to the classroom equipped with his first language or the mother tongue. He is considered a linguistic adult in the sense that by the time he is of the school-going age he is in a position to carry out fundamental communicative functions in the community through his language; he can competently do things at time, in the neighbourhood, at the market-place, in the temple, at the post office and so on. He is equipped with his language and a set of communicative strategies to carry out these functions with considerable efficiency.

It is the usual impression that he has now come to school not for learning any aspect of his spoken language but to learn reading, writing and the literature of his language. This in fact is a false impression. The L_1 learner in the classroom is still only a beginner inspite of his label as an adult. He knows the use of the language, but there are numerous aspects of the communicative dimensions that he needs to acquire. His long years in education contributes to his first language in a number of ways other than the quantum of information he gathers about the language itself and its literature. The following aspects are relevant in the present context :

1. *The Use of Standard Language* : The L_1 classroom helps the learner acquire the standard langauge. Upto the time he came to school the learner had been exposed to one dialect variety or other to which the language of his community belongs. The speech that he had been habituated to contained a large quantity of colloquialism and expressions that cannot be used in formal situations. His schooling now is transforming his speech from the particular dialect variety to the standard variety that is supposed to be spoken and studied in the classroom. This transformation is central to his communicative efficiency as a speaker of the regional or native language. This transition will not be felt in a day or two but takes time for the community to take note of. Once it does he develops a new image that is bound with the acceptability of his language as a school-going speaker of the language.

2. *Use of Polished, Formal Expressions* : The acquisition of the standard language through the classroom exposure helps the learner use polished, formal expressions as part of his new communicative contexts in which he finds himself. The language he used at home was characterised by colloquialism, slangs and dialect expressions not presentable in the company of people who do not belong to the same set up as the speaker. The acquisition of such polished, formal expressions alter his image and give him a greater sense of confidence. Upto this period he carried out his communication chiefly through informal language both at home and outside. Now once in school he begins acquiring more and more formal language and sets in motion a transition that will go on until he will have a thorough command over the formal aspects of the language meant for use in formal communicative situations. Depending on the degree of exposure the individual's language will retain more or less formal language even in informal communicative contexts.

3. *Acquisition of Social Dimensions in Communication* : The L_1 learner in the classroom is now exposed to the communicative strategies of a kind that help him perform better in social situations. Greater exposure to formal communicative contexts enable him now speak his language to suit all sorts of social situations. Exposure to the formal language of the classroom with the textbook as the focus his recognition and expression vocabulary swells in such a way that he has readily on hand words to suit the formal needs of his speech.

4. *Greater Control Over Pace of Speech* : The child's language at home is characterised by irregularity, jerkiness and unwanted pace that often makes his language unintelligible. Once in school the learner is compelled by circumstances to overcome several of his problems of speech as he has to express himself clearly to a large number of students and teachers under varied circumstances. The learner gradually slows down his pace of speech even without conscious efforts and obtain greater control over his language in a variety of ways as acceptable to his peers and teachers. This is an important communicative dimensions in the learning of the first language in the classroom.

5. *Acquisition of Discourse Development Strategies* : Another communicative dimensions of L_1 learning in the classroom is the acquisition of techniques for developing oral as well as written discourses in the language. Developing systematic and organised speech as well as written paragraphs comes with the learning of the L_1. The child is now in a position to think more logically and systematically and can narrate an event or describe a thing with greater control over the speech in general and language in particular. The child acquires a number of discourse development strategies in course of his classroom learning as he is exposed more and more to both formal spoken and formal written language of the school. These and other communicative dimensions of the L_1 classroom indeed highlights our understanding of what constitute the communicative strategies of the L_2 classroom.

3. Communicative Strategies at Work on the L_2 Classroom Peer Exchange

Communicative competence, we have seen, is the built-in ability in the individual speaker that makes him capable of communicating himself effectively to others using what has been called communicative strategies. Communicative strategies in the present context can be viewed from two distinct perspectives : (a) Strategies that are automatically and naturally at work as part of the very learning system including the classroom set up ; and (b) techniques of communication that the teacher will employ in order to create *communicative contexts* in the classroom for students to make communicative use of the language. The present section and the one that follows (Sec. 4) examine in detail what these strategies at work are, and in Sec. 5, we shall examine the classroom techniques for communicative language teaching. The following are the strategies that are at work in peer exchange of language :

1. *Questioning at Work in the Peer Group* : A large variety of contexts arise in the class where automatically and with self motivation students ask questions of their peers. Questioning of this kind arising solely among the peer group is a communicative strategy at work in the class which contribute significantly to the communicative use of English in the classroom. These questions are motivated by a variety of factors. The inquisitive nature of student's work as a principal incentive behind much of the questions that they ask. These may pertain to what their friends do, their teacher's behaviour, the kind of work done in the class and a number of problems they face while responding to the demands of their life in the school. These questions whatever be the motivation at work are a natural resource that can be systematically tapped by the teacher of English for the development and practice in the communicative use of English.

2. *Peer Exchange of Comments and Opinions* : Comments and opinions that often crop up in the classroom among students constitute another communicative strategy that the language employs for its communicative use. The linguistic structure and elements required for questioning and different in thier texture from those required for making comments and expressing opinions in a variety of ways. Peer exchange of comments and opinions create communicative contexts in such a way that the student of English is compelled to acquaint himself with the linguistic structures and devices that enable him to carry out the function with efficiency and ease. As he develops in the use of these strategies, the structures and the strategies he employs becomes more and more complex.

3. *Interpretation of Teacher Feedback* : At the peer group level interpretation of the feedback provided by the teacher from time to time functions as a communicative strategy of great significance. This strategy function chiefly among the bright learner group which is quick to interpret the teacher's attitude to the class as a whole and to individual students in particular. Teachers vary considerably in the nature of their feedback to the performance and behaviour of the class. Some are more prone to give positive feedback while others negative feedback. The nature of the feedback and the frequency with which the feedback is given determine the students' attitude to the class to a great extent. This

interpretation that consistently take place in the classroom is a communicative strategy to enable students make communicative use of the language.

4. *Peer Exchange of Demands and Requests* : Another communicative strategy that functions at the peer level is the peer exchange of demands and requests by means of which communicative use is made of the language. Students have at their level numerous requests and demands to be made. These communicative functions aim at mostly things that need to be done or for exchanging articles of one kind or other among friends. This communicative function employes the structures that are characteristics of requests as well as demands that are so common among students of any level. A lot of language is employed by the pupil when they largely exercise this strategy for making communicative use of the language.

5. *Peer Exchange in Aggressive Situations* : Numerous aggressive situations arise when peer exchange a language becomes necessary. These may be outright quarrels or situations or mere anger when an intention is not realised. These aggressive situations call for a variety of language constructions depending on their nature and students are compelled to use the language to meet these communicative needs in such a way that the degree of language practice to which they are exposed goes up. Peer exchange in aggressive situations is thought of here as a communicative strategy in which communicative use of the language is made using varying structures and vocabulary.

6. *Expression of Emotions* : Numerous situations arise in the classroom when students are compelled to give expression to their emotions in a variety of ways. The expression of emotions is a communicative strategy that enable students use a large variety of structures and lexical items for the purpose and thus make a communicative use of the language. Emotions constitute a complex network whose components are varied and several of these components are often realised in the classroom. The teacher can find out ways of tapping the resources of such contexts to help children make communicative use of English.

Communicative strategies are thus devices seen as at work in communicative contexts of a large variety of kinds where the speaker employs grammatical structures and expressions and lexical items to meet the demands of the contexts. A detailed analysis of classroom situations and those of the school would provide us communicative contexts where the strategies are at work. The few instances or categories we have seen are taken only from one set i.e., exchanges that take place at the peer level. The teacher may not have control over many of these contexts but most of such contexts are at work without direct influence by the teacher. On the other hand, an awareness that communicative strategies are at work in these contexts will help him discover opportunities where he can enhance the communicative use of the language with reference to these contexts.

4. Communicative Strategies at Work : Student-Teacher Exchange

Peer exchange is just one dimension of the communicative strategies at work in the classroom. The second dimension of the communicative strategies at work in the classroom is the student-teacher exchange of language based on the manifold communicative strategies to enable the communicative use of the language. In the case of peer-exchange of communicative language the teacher has often little or no direct control over the contexts, but the student-teacher exchange contexts can be directly controlled by the teacher in a variety of ways. The following are the most basic communicative strategies that are work in the student teacher exchange contexts.

1. *Teacher Initiated Questioning* : The most important of these communicative strategies is the teacher-initiated questioning. During teaching hours and otherwise there arise numerous occasions when the teacher ask a variety of questions. The questioning may be part of the classroom techniques he is using while teaching or the questions may be just enquiry-type and general as part of his general contacts. Whatever be the background of the questioning, here we have an important communicative strategy at work, initiated by the teacher. This strategy creates communicative contexts which have two different functions : first, the students have an opportunity to exercise their listening to communicative language specified with reference to certain structures; second, these questions elicit answers from students. In patterning the response the students employ specific communicative language in which, again, strategies are at work. Teacher initiated questioning is most pervasive and its frequency as a communicative strategy at work is considerable.

2. *Instructions by the Teacher* : Another communicative strategy employed by the teacher consists in all the instructions that the teacher gives from time to time. These instructions may be with specific reference to actual work in the class while teaching or activities that are related to the work in the classroom. Instructions by the teacher make use of grammatical structures of specific kinds and vocabulary of a considerable range. The strategy at work in these instructions has scope for creating numerous communicative contexts of similar kind in which students exercise their listening and speaking skills and obtain practice in the actual communicative use of the language.

3. *Comments and Reprimands* : By virtue of the work he does in the class and teacher is called on to make comments and reprimand students on various occasions as part of his general feedback to the class. The comments and reprimands he makes constitute a communicative strategy for the communicative use of the language in the classroom. Depending on the context and nature of these functions varied grammatical structures and lexical items are made use of by the teacher.

4. *Opinions and Explanations* : Another area where the communicative strategy is at work in a large scale is the giving of opinions and explanations by the teacher using communicative language and thereby creating for the students contexts for the communicative use of the language. Expressing opinions and providing explanations occur both in and outside the scope of regular teaching work. The teacher employs a large number of patterns and lexical items to carryout these functions and thereby provide students an opportunity to listen to the use of the language in a communicative manner. If the teacher is aware of the specific function of such communicative strategies as these, the organisation of both his classroom techniques as well as the use of language for various other purposes can be done in such a way that the classroom will provide maximum exposure of communicative language to the students.

5. Categories of Communication at Work

Communicative language teaching is an approach to classroom teaching with specific reference to the teaching of English as second language where the teaching becomes organised not around the structures of English but on the communicative functions of the language. The teacher as far as possible undertakes a kind of task-oriented teaching where the class has something concrete to do in making the communicative use of the language. Communicative language teaching thus is centred around the communicative functions. These functions are expressed by means of a large number of *communicative categories*. These categories like the strategies that we have examined are moulds highly characterised and specified by communications take place are created by these categories and the contexts become intertwined to enable the communicative use of the language. The following communicative categories can be envisaged as being at work to express the functions that are inherent in the language :

Asking the way

1. Could you tell me the way to the bus station ?
2. Excuse me but, is this is the way to the bus station?
3. How can I reach the bus station, please?
4. Could I know the way to the bus station, please?
5. I wonder if this is the way to the bus station.
6. Do you know the way to the bus station, please
7. Does this road lead to the bus station, please?
8. Am I on the right road to the bus station, please?
9. Please tell me how I can reach the bus station.
10. Kindly show me the way to the bus station.

Apologising

1. I am sorry, please.
2. I am sorry for stepping on your toes.
3. I am awefully sorry for that.
4. Oh, I am really sorry for that.
5. I do not know how to tell you how sorry I feel,

Acceptance

1. I am glad you have invited me to the party.
2. I am grateful you have invited me to the party.
3. We feel obliged for your invitation.
4. Thanks for your invitation.

5. Thank you very much for your kind invitation.
6. Thanks for your concern in inviting us to the party.

Agreement

1. I agree to finish the work by tomorrow.
2. We consent to start for Bombay tomorrow.
3. You have agreed to finish the work by tomorrow.
4. You must agree to finish the work in time.
5. They have agreed that they will meet us tomorrow.

Accusation

1. I am sure you have done it.
2. We feel sure that you are the one who did it.
3. Why are you accusing me of this mistake?
4. They have accused me of a serious crime.
5. What made you do it so badly?
6. How dare you do it at this hour of the day?
7. How could you think of doing it so carelessly?
8. No one else but he has done this nasty work.

Acknowledgment

1. We acknowledge that you are our leader.
2. We know well that you are our leader.
3. We recognise how accomplished a leader you are.
4. They are recognise your leadership already.
5. You must acknowledge how capable he is.
6. We are sure you will do the work well for us.

Admonition

1. We warn you never again to repeat it.
2. I warned him twice about the lapse.
3. You should be very careful about your involvement.
4. They have informed him how dangerous his work is.
5. I tell you, you will suffer for it.

6. Why do you do it over and over again?

Affirmation

1. We declare that John is the real culprit.
2. I assert again that she will marry him.
3. They have maintained their stand once again,
4. I do not know if they will ever change their opinion.
5. I say for certain that he will come back soon.

Consequence

1. Do you know what will happen after this?
2. I know how he is going to react now.
3. Consequently, they have decided to leave.
4. As a consequence, I had to suffer much.
5. Let him remain in the prison because he deserves it.

Contrast

1. As against this, I would prefer going there.
2. In contrast to what he said, see what has happened?
3. If this is too simple, you can take up that work.
4. What is the difference between the two people?
5. How different the two books are ?

Certainty

1. I am indeed certain that he will win the election.
2. John is sure to win the election.
3. They are certain to go to war in a short time.
4. Make sure that he pays it up.
5. Are you convinced that he is the right man?
6. John is convinced of my innocence.

Comparison

1. John is taller than Seema.
2. I should now try harder for a wain.
3. Why do you speak louder than necessary?

4. Compared to what you said, he had told me a lie.
5. There is no comparison to this model of the house.

Expressing Emotions

1. How sad I feel you do not know!
2. I am overwhelmed by your concern for me.
3. Oh! How hard I tried, yet success is far off.
4. I am glad to meet you, my friend.
5. John is sorry for all that you did to him.
6. I love you so much, my son.

Explanation

1. To put it clearly, you have to work harder.
2. As far as the details are concerned, one needs to enquire further.
3. We should explain it to him further.
4. Why don't you give us the details?
5. I do not know how I shall account for it.

Emphasizing

1. This is indeed the truth.
2. You cannot do it any other way.
3. I am convinced you can do the work.
4. The fact is that you failed to meet him.
5. John is certainly not responsible for the accident.

Frequency

1. They do it quite often.
2. Never have seen him do it.
3. They frequently visited the place.
4. I was always after him for that work.
5. They seldom come to visit me.

Insistence

1. I want you to complete the work today itself.
2. He insists that I should leave the place.

3. Make sure that he leaves the place.
4. At any cost you should get the work done.
5. You should keep the money only in your purse.

Invitation

1. We have been invited to see the factory.
2. You are most cordially invited to see the factory.
3. Please come to see my factory.
4. You are most welcome to my factory.
5. I am pleased to invite to the party.

Promises

1. I promise to give you the money in a week's time.
2. I shall meet you on Monday at any cost.
3. They have promised to complete the work.
4. Promise that you will never repeat it!
5. Why don't you promise to visit my place?

Permission

1. You may buy those clothes.
2. You can buy him a doll.
3. May I come in, please ?
4. Can I borrow some money from him?
5. John is permitted to visit Britain.

Questioning

1. Have you broken these glasses?
2. Tell me, If you have broken these glasses.
3. How much time would you take to do the work?
4. Why are you questioning me like this?
5. Where have your friends gone today?

6. Classroom Techniques for Communicative Teaching

Communicative approach to classroom teaching equips the teacher of English with a set of classroom techniques to implement its principles.

We may call these *Communicative techniques* for classroom teaching or techniques for communicative teaching. Within the methodological framework of communicative language teaching, the teacher in the classroom decides to organise a set of techniques for the learner 'to do things in English' and to learn communicative functions in the use of English. These techniques are apart from and are to be coordinated to the communicative strategies that are *at work* in the classroom atmosphere as seen in detail in Sections 2 and 3. The following classroom techniques can be recommended for the teaching of communicative Categories just as we have techniques for the teaching of the structures of English within the framework of a structural syllabus :

1. *Group work* has been thought of as one the best methods for initiating communicative activities. There is no end to the variety of techniques that can form part of the group method of teaching. The objective is to help the leaners use the new language function on communicative category in a small group, talk to one another, ask questions, find patterns that will constitute the correct new *language function* on *communicative category* in a small group, talk to one another, ask questions, find patterns that will constitute the correct answers, reorganise the answers for the use of different patterns, and practice the use of communicative categories that are essentially part of conversational English. Expressions and polite forms such as the following should form part of the learner's language through group activities : Good morning, Sir ; what can I do for you? How can I be of help to you? Could you tell me what the matter is? I wonder what I can do for you; Just a minute, Sir; Excuse me, but....; Certainly, Sir; Just a minute, please; Could you pass that book to me, please? Would you want me to come with you to the shop? Is there anything that I can do for you? May I have your pen for a while? Well, I don't think I can tell you this; I don't know if I should tell you this; You are most welcome to join us; Can I take leave of you, please? I think I must join you later... the list of such communicative expressions can be endless. Communicative language teaching enables the teacher to take care of such find shades of what we have called the communicative act.

2. *Pair work* is another very effective device for initiating communicative activities. Here the class will be divided into groups of two as they are seated in the class. No rearrangements becomes necessary and a lot of time is saved on that account. Interquestioning as a technique

is the best for pair work. One will ask the question based on the materials given and the second will provide the answer. Then they swap roles and do the same. The teacher can workout other techniques for pair work to provide communication practices.

3. *Role Play* constitutes another dynamic technique that lies at the core of communicative language teaching. The individual in society is essentially a role player. Language is employed as a vehicle to give expression to these roles in a variety of ways. These natural roles in social life and simulated in communicative language teaching, in the classroom, and the learner uses language to give expression to the same features of experience.

4. *Dramatisation* includes a variety of activities right from simple enactment of a piece of conversation upto some form of a skirt in which a whole short these can behandled. This is highly activity oriented. The language function that has newly been introduced can be enlarged and worked out into some form of dramatisation. While role play is simple dramatisation can be complex. In either case the important aspect is the communicative function that is practical.

5. *Miming* : while miming and role play have things in common, miming can generate greater fun of worked out well; In mining as a classroom technique one or more students engage in a process of imitating some character, say, a barber, a smith, a doctor, a typist, etc. This can be any imitation or simple action translated into language by other students.

6. *Reporting Observation* : There are many ways of carrying out communicative activities by reporting observations of several kinds. This is a highly practical activity. The learners can be asked to (a) measure the size of things, rooms, and compound sand report the measurement in English, (b) Calculate or solve problem and report thier findings in English, (c) observe game and sports and report to the class the details, (d) observe nature and report to the class about a field, riverside or picnic spot, (e) observe and report the traffic, (f) observe and report experiment in the laboratory.

7. *Interquestioning* : Questioning is a classroom technique that the teacher himself employes, while interquestioning is the same activity done by the pupils with a different purpose. A group work or a pair work can integrate this technique. While both group work or pair work does not enable the whole class to listen to a student's question or the answer,

interquestioning goes on before and for the whole class. The teacher will work on how this technique should be carried out and what material should be used for the purpose.

Apart from the above communicative techniques we may envisage : 8. *Work on Pictures*, 9. *Work on Models*, 10. *Making a guess*, 11. *Taking about John*, 12. *Listen a Say using the tape recorder*, 13. *Reporting Television or video scenes*, and 14. *The use of the overhead projector*. Pictures can provide the basis for communicative work. Model can be used for students to talk. A packet can be passed in the class, for instance, and the class can made guesses. Ramesh can describe a few things about John. Television programmes and scenes from the video can be the springboard for language work. Recorded dialogues can be the basis for large-scale communicative language activity. These are only a few instances of the great potential communicative language teaching has in generating classroom techniques. The teacher should be able to view these communicative strategies at work in thier own way in the classroom, and the communicative technique that the teacher will employ for the communicative use of the language and achieve a synthesis of these two-dimensions.

7. Linking the Classroom with the Community

Language is the unique factor that keeps the community going. Just as language is the embodiment of a community's sociocultural life, the community at large is the foundation on which language thrives, the interdependence of langauge and community is so great that both becomes the sides of the same coin. It is against this background that we should view the classroom where language is taught. The class is a representative or miniature community which is formally structured to imbibe all aspects of the life of the community. As such the teacher in the classroom should seen his work as that of a mediator whose principal aim it is to link the classroom with the community and thereby enables the learner *harmonise his relation* with the community.

The learner is drawn from the community for his classroom learning and the teacher must be aware of the fact that he is to be given back to the community after having helped him develop his potentials for the roles that he will play as an adult. The teacher should therefore ensure that learning should take place in the classroom in the same communicativers contexts as those found as part of the life of the community. This is particularly true of the teaching of languages. The native speakers of a language employs the language in countless communicative situations. Each such situation consists of numerous communicative contexts we have been talking about. Each communicative context further consists of a series of communicative events that are definable with reference to the language constructions at use of the speaker and this listener.

Translations at the post office may be thought of a communicative situation for present purposes. In sociologistics one would define it as a social situation of a broad dimension. The *transactions at the post office* can then be thought of in terms of a sequence of communicative contexts. Buying stamps may be thought of as a communicative context. If the process of buying stamps occur in a few phases each phase may be thought of as a communicative act; it happens in one unified phase the context in this particular case will be an act with mutually exclusive dimensions. The teacher of English with a correct understanding of the nature of such communicative contexts will orient his classroom teaching in terms of such communicative contexts.

A link between the community and the classroom can be established by drawing *examples and materials* from community life. In communicative language teaching the emphasis on take is considerably. We have called it task oriented teaching. The task for the pursual of the class will be drawn from instances related to actual life in the community. The textbook is prepared with an eye on the community conscious of the proposed for which the institutional materials are based on life-experience drawn from the Community. This in several ways increases the communicative dimension and task centred teaching of language in the classroom.

In different ways the learner in the classroom should be lead out of the textbook centered learning in the classroom, to the midst of actual community life. The school can make arrangement for such *community experience* mostly in an informal manner and thus enhance the scope of outdoor learning of the language. Community experiences increase the learner's enthusiasms, increase their level of motivation for purposeful learning and add a new dimension to the scope of learning. These community experiences can have greater scope wherever these can have deeper socio-cultural implications. Language is a socio-cultural phenomenon; as such we shall be in a position to remake concrete social and cultural elements from the life of the community to constitute material for learning. A concrete realisation of this way be difficult with reference to English but what we are saying is true of any second language learning situation for that matter. Socio-cultural factors relevant to a particular community will form the material for the learning of the structures and the vocabulary of the second language. A teacher who is one the look out for such factors related to the life of the community will find ample material to form the basis for the preparation of instructional material to supplement the textbook.

Another aspect of the relation between the classroom and the community is the *informal language.* Informal use of the language is inherent in the life of the community. An analysis of actual communicative situations in the life of a community will show that it is the informal language that go into the making of a vast majority of these situations. By informal language we mean that language which the member of a community speaks at all informal situations such as at home, in friends circles and at places where langauge, and the teacher is habituated to the use of former only. It becomes necessary for the teacher to introduce himself to aspects of informal English, for instance, if he is not already conversant with these, and then use these in his classroom teaching. The teacher can have a pool of infernal experience that are part of the speech habits of the native communicative and use this pool of expressions in the teaching of English.

Introducing *informal language* into the classroom would mean primarily looking for simple counterparts of the big words that we are usually habituated to not only in writing but also in speech. The informal counterparts of the following words are for instance paired with them : Commence : begin, continue: keep up, conclude; and, discover;, find out, explode; blow up, encounter; come across, invent; make up, enter; go in (to), tolerate; put up with, investigate; look into, surrender: give in, wear: put on and so on. In most cases the Indian speaker of English has access move to the formal usage than the informal one and seldom is any difference made between our expressions in speech and in writing. Our classroom work can improve significantly if the teacher is exposed to the informal (colloquial) variety of English and provide communicative use of English in the classroom.

Again, as part of his attempt to undertake communicative teaching of the language the teacher can experience his mind to teach the language by getting *community situation enacted* in the classroom. He may resort to demonstrative and dramatisation techniques which will help enact community situations to have communicative use of the language in the classroom. The teacher can get students work out a list of such situations for use in the classroom distributing these in teaching and practicing different language functions and grammatical structures.

Communicative language teaching, as we have seen throughout the foregoing pages, focuses on the communicative use of the language just as the native speakers employ the language for a variety of communicative purposes. The communicative use of the language employes a variety of communicative strategies that we have examined which are seen as at work in the communicative contexts. These in turn go into the making of communicative situations that are broad social situations which occur in the community and keep the community going. The communicative contexts are again seen as collective instances of communicative acts. In several cases these contexts and acts have identical extension depending on the social context we are referring to. The teacher of English needs to be aware of these communicative dimensions as worked out on the preceding pages and organise his classroom practices with greater originally, creativeness and efficiency. He must be thoroughly acquainted with the techniques of communicative classroom teaching so that the students will make the best use of the resources for their own language development. Such a systematic understanding of the communicative dimensions of language alone can help the teacher do this.

7

A NEW APPROACH TO CLASSROOM INTERACTION

1. Fundamentals of Classroom Interaction

Interaction has been the catch word in educational psychology for several decades and research has gone into all conceivable perspectives of this phenomenon that lies at the very centre of all classroom practices. Interaction is a factor very fundamental to the structure and practices of classrooms at all levels of education. It is also a factor that controls the working of all classroom techniques through which the teacher organises his teaching there is no approach to classroom teaching which in some way or other place a high premium on classroom interaction as a principal medium for the realisation of learning.

Interaction essentially is some kind of an exchange between two or more individuals with an overt or covert (implicit) purpose on hand. The exchange may be verbal or non verbal, short or prolonged ,resulting in a positive or negative experience. Interaction can be *unidirectional* or *bidirectional* (mutual) with only one individual providing the stimulus situation and other functioning as a passive listener or recipient, or it can be with two or more individuals ,as in the latter case, both providing the stimulus and actively responding to the stimuli. In both the cases interaction takes place at different degrees to be defined with reference to the attitude of the recipient.

In other words interaction is a stimulus-response situation with some degree of verbal or non -verbal exchange that would result in positive or negative feeling in the individuals who function as the agent of the interaction. Learning and interaction are mutually definable since all learning situations have some element of interaction involved as well as all interactional situations result in some degree of learning in its broadest definition. Interaction is a creative and productive factor as even elementary forms of interaction that happen among human individuals involve intellectual and imaginative organisation of elements involved in the interactional situation.

Interactional situations may have an overt or implicit purpose on hand. Philosophically and psychologically speaking all human actions have a purpose of an overt or covert kind. Viewing interaction on a basis narrower than this we find that the individuals who interact with each other have a purpose that at the time of interaction may not be present in their conscious mind. If the purpose is consciously present in the minds of the individuals, the interaction, however, short living it may be, will have a higher degree of intensity. Interaction of very high intensity and elevated purpose are called *Communion*, or *interpersonal Communion*. This notion is irrelevant for present purposes.

The notion of interaction, therefore, is most relevant to the classroom. The classroom is a miniature society which functions with definite direction's and a purpose. The classroom has a definite structure that has much to do with the realisation of classroom interaction. The nation of interaction is intrinsic to the functioning of the classroom. Interaction when applied to the structure and functioning of the classroom would mean any *definable exchange* that happens between two or more learners or between the learner and the teacher. *Learner interaction* or what is known as peer interaction is one major dimension of classroom interaction and *learner-teacher interaction* is another. All classroom interaction can be explained under these two major heads. Interaction of one kind or other, of one dimension or other becomes the serious preoccupation of teachers of all subjects in relation to effective teaching practices. All such problems may be traced to various dimensions of classroom interaction: 1. The psychological dimensions, 2. The sociological dimensions, and 3. The linguistic dimensions of classroom interaction. The three together will give us a total perspective of the relevance and problems of classroom interaction as a major factor in teaching.

2. Psychological Dimensions of Classroom Interaction

Classroom interaction needs to be understood as a psychological factor in order to have the right perspective of its role in the development of the learner in the classroom in general and in the learning of a second language in particular. Interaction is basically a psychological factor and needs to viewed with reference to other factors and needs to be viewed with reference to other factors in psychology that determine classroom learning. Interaction is a process involving individuals, situations and other factors coordinated together to produce an event with its purpose its nucleus. Interaction is a psychological factor because human individuals are involved and it is defined within the scope of the behaviour of the individual. It becomes a sociological phenomenon where interaction is defined with reference to the behaviour of the individual in a social context. It becomes a linguistic phenomenon when the communicative, verbal comment of interaction is seen as the focus against which interaction can be analysed and studied. The three dimensions are indeed complementary to one another and are based on the ultimate explanation of interaction as an event.

1. Interaction and Motivation. There is a definite relationship between classroom interaction and motivation. Motivation is one of the fundamental psychological factors at work behind learning. The two closely interact in the context of second language learning in the classroom .The student finds himself in a characteristic situation marked by problems, needs for adjustment etc. Even the highly motivated and independent student looks upon the peer group for support in times of difficulty . Interaction both at the peer level and at the student-teacher level comes as a basic help in the student's adjustment to the language classroom .

The teacher by creating interactional atmosphere can enhance the motivation of the bright learner, the average learner and the slow learner in various degrees. The bright student will employ classroom interaction to meet his elements for challenge and leadership; he derives considerable satisfaction from being able to talk to the class and do things for the class. The average student will increase his confidence in coping with the learning requirements of the classroom and try to improve the quality of his work because he has to face the class in several interactional situations. Interactional for the slow learner comes as a boom because he will be thereby compelled to participate in the mainstream of the classwork. Interaction thus functions as a principal device in providing added motivation to all factions of the class.

2. *Interaction and Achievement:*Classroom interaction is the environment in which student achievement is realised and enhanced. The student who is capable of taking benefit of the interactional situations that are created or that naturally arise in the class have the advantage of an increased level of achievement. This is true especially in the learning of languages where greater exposure functions as a factor for achievement of the components of language. Peer interaction helps mutual clarification ideas and aspects as well as develop in them the art of readily exchanging and discussing these ideas and aspects of content mater with other students in the class. Student-teacher interaction develops in students the habit of participating in discussions and question-answer sessions and thereby deep an eye on the achievement side of this learning.

Interaction and achievement are closely linked in the learning of a second language. A class that is activity-centred and interaction-oriented has great scope for the learning, practice and use of the language and feel satisfied because of the level of achievement the class is able to secure in one way or other. Students performance in the class is itself an indicator of the level of achievement. Here interaction functions both a means to and a measure of achievement.

3. *Interaction and Memory:* Classroom interaction is one way or other on overt, concrete and perceptible phenomenon which students even as silent spectators take benefit from. Memory as a psychological factor of learning depends on the learning stimuli being overt, concrete and perceptible .The more concrete and organised the material is the better will it be impressed in the minds of the learner whatever his age may be. Learning through abstractions which do not involve concrete and dependable images for the learner to hang on leaves the learner's memory in doldrums. When learning involves concreteness i.e. concrete images, especially visual images or auditory images of varying kind, the material hangs on in his memory. This is true of all the components of memory: the intake component, the retention component and the recall component of memory. What classroom interaction does is to provide learning with this concreteness of all dimensions and help the student associate abstract categories with concrete visual and auditory images.

The language classroom exploits this relationship in a significant manner. The second language is presented to the learner not only as mere listening, speaking, reading and writing. These skills are constantly employed as the medium for a high degree of abstractions especially at the level of language categories, rules of use and usage, and the complete structure of meanings which are presented to the learner. The concrete language skills are only the medium for the acquisition of these abstractions. All aspects of classroom interaction, at the level of classroom techniques or outside this scope ,aim at making concrete this world of abstractions and thereby help the learner understand, retain and recall with case the abstract categories which are at the very core of language learning. Classroom interaction thus constitutes the very foundation of the learner's memory which in turn is central to language learning.

4. *Interaction and Imagination :* Classroom interaction provides a concrete basis for the students imagination to function the way it should. Learning in general and acquisition of knowledge in particular is a process of acquisition and organisation of conceptual units into mental constructs. Levels of concreteness take place in this world abstractions with the corresponding organisation of mental images which we call imagination. These images need not necessarily be visual images; they are fed into human imagination by all the sensory perceptions of man. Hence our imagination works on visual, auditory, factory and tactile images fed into the faculty by our sense experiences.

Classroom interaction becomes the principal feeding ground for the development of the learner's imagination. The teacher is thus expected to provide optimum coordination of conceptual units with sense images through sensory experiences in the classroom. The teacher who uses a picture or an object to teach the meaning of a grammatical structure or a vocabulary item is infact catering to this need of the learner for a sensory basis for the matter he is learning. Classroom interaction can introduce into the classroom a variety of sense perceptions for the learner to hang on interaction can be based on the use of pictures, actions or illustrations and demonstrations of any kind.

The language has considerable applications of the relationship seen above. Language learning becomes a hazardous task when the teacher has no concrete images equivalent to a particular notion to place before the class. The teacher of grammar both formal and functional, and the teaching of textual items should be based on concrete images for the learner's imagination to depend on. The teacher who finds out ways and means of providing these parallel experiences principally through effective classroom interaction will succeed in putting across his material most effectively .

5. *Interaction and Creativity :* Classroom interaction is a fundamental factor in developing and exploiting students creative ability. Creativity is viewed as the individual's endowment to organise his environment in such a way as to produce new and meaningful experiences . It is primarily an endowment, a gift of nature to man to live above his animal nature. Thus every individual has some degree of creative ability as a man. The difference lies in this degree of endowment as in the case of pure intelligence. But the difference as we experience it in individuals comes chiefly from the individual's degree of exposure to an environment that permits and encourages the development of this ability. The greater such environment is the better the development of creative intelligence.

Language learning is more and more understood as a creative experience. The present-day transformational generative grammar gas enhanced our understanding of the role of creativity in language acquisition and production. The classroom is expected to create adequate second language atmosphere which constitutes the back-ground for the student to interaction the various components of language . The student's languages competence depends fully on this exposure and the internalisation. In this process classroom interaction plays the most fundamental role. The exposure and internalisation will take place only if the peer interaction and student-teacher interaction will take place in the classroom. The more the language is used in speech and in writing in the classroom both by the students and the teacher the greater will be the exposure and internalisation of the second language.

Apart from these aspects related to the internalisation of language components, other aspects of creativity are based on classroom interaction. When classroom interaction is adequate the student finds himself in a challenging situation in which there occurs greater student involvement and participation. Such an involvement by the class at large adds to the enthusiasm of the bright, average and slow learner groups to such a considerable degree that each of the groups will be compelled to exert themselves to pay attention, involve themselves, give answers and take part in activities. This is the environment that creativity requires for its development. The individual then, manipulates, organises and attempts to respond to this productive environment. This contributes to the development of his creativity in a significant way. The teacher needs to understand and be aware of the role interaction plays thus and organise his reaching in this direction.

6. *Interaction and Skills:* The development of any skill forming part of classroom teaching has its basis on classroom interaction. By skills is meant in general any component of human behaviour that can be acquired and developed only through certain well-defined habits. Skills and habit formation are the sides of the same coin. Skills vary from manipulatory skills to language and academic skills of several kinds to which the classroom contributes. (See Monograph 10 for details Reference skills). The development of all skills depend chiefly on the intensity of the practice that goes into. Practice means many things. Learning typewriting as such dies not require the presence of other people. But this is not the case with language skills.

Classroom interaction and language skills are interrelated. Language skills are mainly listening, speaking, reading, and writing appreciation and discourse Development. In the development of many skills the presence of other individuals to speak, to listen to and to participate becomes necessary. In otherwords as in the case of (2.5) exposure to the language on the one hand and the atmosphere to use the language by the individual on the other becomes absolutely necessary. Classroom interaction comes to focus in such instance. Interaction provides the background and the atmosphere for the development of the listening-speaking skills of language because the method makes no provision for active classroom interaction in which to use the language.

7. *Interaction and Communication:* Communication is most fundamental as a psychological factor in the development of personality. The learner in the classroom is placed in that situation in order to achieve maximum interaction and thereby achieve communication with other members of the community. This communication with the teacher and the peer group is the feeding ground for acquisition of information, skills and change in behaviour. The whole process is psychological because therein individuals interact, new forms of behaviour pattern are realised and the atmosphere contributes significantly to the development of the learner's personality.

Language is communication (See. Monograph 6.) . It is verbal communication. For the development of second language the teacher needs to create interactional situations which become communicative context. A communicative act is defined with reference to the speaker, listener and the message that is communicated. These three components made a communicative act unique in several ways. The success of such an act depends on the disposition of the speaker and the listener and the unity of the message that is communicated. The teacher in the classroom can have control over these three components of communication. Classroom interaction is again the feeding ground for the realisation of such communicative acts whereby effective learning of the language will take place. In the context of the classroom an interactional situation is conceived of as broader than a communicative act. Interactional situations can therefore contribute the background of acts of communication in which to learn the language.

8. *Interaction and Behaviour Change:* The learner in the classroom is placed in that situation to develop his manifold manipulative and language skills, to develop his quantum of information about the world around, and to bring about desirable change in his behaviour. Classroom interaction forms the background against which such behavioral changes take place. Interaction is a process by which individuals communicate to each other one way or other which involves some form an exchange . This communication involves the mental faculties of the individual, his aptitudes and attitudes in varying degrees. This involvement contributes to the development of these faculties in such a way that this development is reflected in the individual's behaviour pattern undergoes change in desired detections primarily because of the interaction that he manages to establish with other individuals.

Classroom interaction, again, enhances the student's *exposure to the world outside*. The world view that the individual develops takes place with reference to the persons that he comes to contact from time to time. The class is the centre of the individual students life experiences, and the world view that he develops depends thus on the exposure that he has to other individuals in the class, at home and out in the community. Classroom interaction i.e., listening to the teacher and the peer group provides him with a frame work in which to organise his life experiences. The student's view of the would begins in the classroom and interaction is the feeding ground for this world view too.

The psychological dimensions of classroom interaction thus function as the chief perspective from which we can view the development of the student in general and his language development in particular. Interaction at its core is personal communication in which behaviour in general and language in particular are shaped. In each of the psychological factors we have examined interaction functions in turn as the feeding ground or the spring board for the development of the student's personality in general and second language learning in particular. A knowledge of these factors should help the teacher function effectively in the classroom .

3. Language-Specific Interactional Situations

Classroom interaction is seen as a concrete factor that contributes significantly to all aspects of the student's development and in particular language development. There are aspects of classroom interaction over which the teacher has no control and this happens mostly at the peer interaction level. But among the most definable interactional situations a sizeable group may be called *language specific interactional situations* and the rest could be called content-specific *interactional situations.* The teacher can control and guide the following interactional situations in the teaching of a second language like English:

1. *Presentation*: Presentation is a step in second language teaching which will be considered a single interactional situation and involves numerous *interactional* acts. An interactional act is the smallest unit of interaction that can be thought of. Presentation becomes relevant in the teaching of speech grammar, vocabulary, and poetry. Presentation is also relevant in the teaching of all non-language subjects in the sense that whatever is the content matter of a unit needs to be presented to the class one way or other. Presentation essentially is that step in teaching when the teacher makes the class understand a unit of content matter using one or more adequate techniques. A number of interactional acts constitute the presentation step:

(a) Stray questioning of a variety of kind can create interaction during the presentation of grammar, vocabulary or content matter. Here it is called stray because questioning is <u>not used</u> as the main technique. Questioning is used in the above cases only to find out occasionally if the work is going home, as well as to involve the students in the work especially if the presentation is done by means of verbal illustration. This introduces some degree of variety and involvement at this stage.

(b) Context cues can be provided to the class which will elicit questions from students. These context cues will constitute part of demonstrative or illustrative work that the teacher undertakes. A sentence may be constructed as a model sentence in such a way that it will make the bright learner ask questions. Providing cues will be more relevant in content -centred teaching of non-language subjects.

(c) Pictorial illustration is capable of bringing about considerable degree of classroom interaction as part of presentation. The picture is presented to the class and the teacher works on a grammatical item, vocabulary or a relevant poem. Again instead of outright questions the class should be given cues in such a way that the students should come out with comments or questions. The purpose of the picture here is to illustrate the meaning and use of a particular language item or to illustrate the meaning of a content unit in the case of subjects. The picture will in turn result in classroom interaction.

(d) Interaction during presentation also would mean using the material on the blackboard as the spring board for activity on the part of the students. Questions, comments and clarification are the chief means of interaction at this level . Depending on the level at which the teacher works, there would be greater or less degree of exchange between the teacher and the class, particular the affluant group of students in the class.

(e) Presentation of materials can take place via audio-visual devices such as the tape-recorder on the one hand, and the video on the other. The recorder does the presentation through auditory modality and the video does so through the audio-visual modalities. The teacher can join the class at this stage and interact with the class through questions, comments and clarification. Since the presentation takes place through the technological media, the teacher can use his energy in achieving productive and creative interaction with the students in a very careful manner at the time of the presentation of the material.

2. *Drill as an Interactional Situation:* Drill is a step in second language teaching that aims at a definite type of practice. The practice that drill aims at is usually known as mechanical or automatic practice. The step of drill tries to acquaint the student's with the form, formal organisation, both spoken form and written form of the structural item, sentence pattern or the vocabulary. Because of this unique features of this stage, it is susceptible to much classroom interaction. Drill is a

highly language specific interactional situation in which a high degree of the repetition of these formal units is involved with a view to forming relevant habits. The following interactional acts constitute drill:

(a) Visual presentation of language material on the chalkboard, or on an overhead projector functions as the stimulus for interactional situation. The teacher guides the production of sentences from a substitution table or a pattern by individual students. This is a teacher-initiated interactional situation. Students construct sentences using the pattern based on the cues the teacher gives or forms sentences using the substitution table or as in the case of practice for vocabulary merely reads out the sentences in which the new words are used.

(b) Oral presentation of language material by the teacher himself or using the record player functions as the stimulus for the production of sentences by individual pupils. This interactional act helps students listen to and repeat the sentences in which the language items are made use of. While visual presentation takes care of the written form of the material , oral presentation alone or along with the visual-material takes care of the spoken form of the language material.

(c) Drill as an interactional situation can also employ chorus work. The teacher guides repetition of the visually or orally presented language material by a small group of sex or eight students or by a row of students or by the whole class. The smaller the group of students involved at a time in the repetition the better effect of the drill.

(d) Drill has also other interactional acts involved in it. The teacher provides a variety of teed back at this step which establish contact between he himself and the student as an individual or the class as a whole. Corrections of the repeated elements, positive feedback using cues like 'yes or all right', negative feedback such as facial expressions or words that indicate that the teacher is not happy with the answer etc. go into the particular interactional situation. Drill as an interactional situations has the potential for student involvement of a very controlled type as described above.

3. *Meaningful / Communicative Practice* as an interactional situation. Drill takes care of establishing habits in the spoken form and written form of the language item. Second language teaching is centred on the meaningful and communicative practice takes care of the actual use of the language item in meaningful situation (not merely repetition of formal

units), communicative practice aims at the students use of the language item in communicative purposes. The two aspects are considered one in the present context for practical purposes. The following interactional acts can be envisaged as part of this interactional situation :

(a) The technique of questioning is central to meaningful / communicative practice. Questioning involves a student-teacher interactional act. This is the step when questioning as a technique is used in a most meaningful way for discussion-oriented purposes. These questions are based on communication centred situations or what has been called communicative situations in general and communicative contexts in particular. If this interactional situation can be turned into a discussion with students asking questions of each other and of the teacher, we have made the best use of this interactional situation for communicative purposes.

(b) Group method is regarded as one of the best ways of organising this step with several technique that can go into its making (Monograph no. 2). The unique texture of group method is based on its high degree of interactional potential i.e. ability to create interaction among the students. Group method employs a large variety of techniques such as interquestioning, dramatisation, language games, the use of language steps and so on. All these techniques bring about a fair degree of exchange between individuals, make them communicate, talk to each other, feel the pulse of communicative language. The teacher will supervise the group activities with the principal aim of creating optimum and well organised interactional acts.

(c) Dramatisation without group work is another technique that the teacher uses to create interaction. Dramatisation can be based on dialogues available in the textbook, those prepared by the teacher or simple cats to be enacted by the students, orally guided by the teacher. Dramatisation has the potential to involve two or a group of students which can in turn be repeated with other groups of students.

(d) Language games of a variety of kinds, again, can be used to create interaction to provide communicative use of the language. These language games create also an atmosphere of fun which in turn will motivate the students to involve themselves better in the work.

4. *Discourse Construction(Oral)* :An oral composition can be taught

with a very high degree of classroom interaction. Hence it can be thought of as an interactional situation. The teacher step builds the material of the composition. Interaction is based on the sequence of questions that he asks. In affluent classes these question can create an atmosphere of discussion with students participating in the question-answer process. A composition is unique because of its discourse development characteristic. This is the only lesson where the individual works on a full discourse unit of the language. The teacher has also occasions for providing a high degree of feedback because of the active student involvement that this interactional situation is capable of.

5. *Discourse Construction(Written)* : A written composition can be organised with a fair degree of classroom interaction. Because of its potential for some interaction it can be called an interactional situation. The teacher builds the material of the composition exactly the same way as he does with the oral composition, through sequential questioning which can take the form of a discussion if students are also capable of working independently and asking questions. The difference lies when the discourse will at the end be constructed orally by individual students in oral composition, avoiding this they undertake the writing of the discourse after the discussion step. The teacher's guidance in several ways during the time of writing again, creates interactional acts of very useful kind.

Again, work on pronunciation, silent reading, reading aloud by the pupils, recitation of poetry, practice in pre-writing skills, work on spellings and punctuation have the potential for the different degrees of classroom interaction. In each of the above cases the teacher has to consciously manipulate the interactional acts to make them most effective to suit the particular purpose on hand as well as to enhance classroom interaction for its own sake. The interactional situation envisaged above are language-specific situations that are in fact identical to step in teaching various kinds of lessons. The chief purpose in this context is to make the teacher of a second language like English as well as teachers of other non-language subjects to be aware of the areas in classroom teaching that can offer optimum classroom interaction. The perspective of interaction is considered with a focus so that even teachers who do not teach English or other language will create an awareness of the great potential of classroom interaction for effective teaching.

4. Content-specific Interactional Situations

Interactional situations are conceived of as language-specific and content-specific depending on the specific purpose for which the interactional situation is created. We shall examine in general in the present section what constitutes the content-specific interactional situations. These are envisaged keeping in mind non-language subjects which are content-oriented except courses and subjects which are content-oriented except courses and subjects that teach a skill such as tailoring or type-writing. Even in such courses the theory component is content-specific . Content-specific courses employ a variety of techniques to put across a given *quantum of information* about *a component of theory or* a *component of practice*. Classroom interaction or an interactional situation is employed as a means to (a) present the new content matter (organised information) (b) consolidate the knowledge of the given content matter and (c) revise the knowledge of the material. In a regular classroom organisation the revision of previously taught material may be the starting point, followed by the presentation of the new material and then a variety of ways of consolidating the knowledge of the information. The following interactional situations could be thought of in the present context:

(a) *Questioning* is used as the principal technique for the revision of a previously taught unit of content matter, say, in geography. The questions are content-based and aim at answers from the class rising information that the already taught unit contains . The questions do not aim at any kind of practice that may be the case with language-specific lessons.

(b) *Reading aloud* from the textbook to present the new unit of content-matter is a technique widely used in content-specific teaching. This becomes an interactional situation when the teacher stops in between, poses a question, makes a comment, gives an explanation, asks a question, invites a question based on a given cue, attempts to establish a link between the past units and the present one. The degree of interaction depends on the level at which the students can make a comment, ask a question, make a clarification, answer a question, correct another student's answer are statement and so on.

(c) *The lecture form of presentation* using the narrative technique without reading from the text is a method of subjects in schools. The lecture method of presentation (See Monograph No. 1) has numerous ways of combining with it techniques that are essentially interactional by nature. The same techniques mentioned /above as part of reading aloud from the textbook (4.b.) are applicable in this method too. The lecture method of presentation assumes the level of an interactional situation depending on the number of interactional acts the teacher is able to integrate with the method.

(d) *Seminar method* can be introduced in the classroom for presenting new content with a view to providing interactional situation. Here two or three students can be helped to prepare a new unit. These students can be asked to read some prepared material for the class. This will be followed by a question-answer session which the teacher can exploit for initiating considerable degree of interaction (See Monograph. No. 3).

(e) *An overhead projector* comes handy in presenting content-matter centred around a diagram, a model, an outline or a picture. The projection in the classroom is used as the basis for a great degree of classroom interaction. Numerous interactional acts such as questioning, explanation, comments, interquestioning (between pupils), description by pupils etc. can be centred on the projection. The teacher can carefully organise these interactional acts.

(f) *Group method* can be applied by content-specific classes for consolidation and revision of the unit already introduced. After the teacher's work of presentation of the new unit the class can be yoked to group tasks. Numerous techniques that can go with group method (Monograph. No. 2) can be employed to initiate optimum interaction in the group work.

5. Guiding Interactional Situations in the Classroom

An effective teacher in the classroom places a high premium on optimum student involvement by creating interactional situations of the kind we have seen so far. In several cases these situations occur simply by virtue of the techniques the teacher uses from time to time depending on the nature of the lesson he is teaching. The techniques are such that a certain degree of student involvement occurs without the teacher being conscious of it or without manipulating the classroom situation in any special direction.

An effective teacher on the other hand has definite ways of guiding the class activities in such a way that he caters to the interactional needs of the class. This conscious awareness of the need for creating interactional situations in general and interactional acts in particular takes the teacher a long way ahead in making his classroom practices effective. The teacher looks for avenues within his classroom techniques to introduce an interactional act and get adequate student participation. He will keep the three different groups in the class in mind: the bright learner, the average learner and the slow learner. With a little encouragement or by merely offering a chance the bright student can be made to ask a question, make a comment, explain a problem, describe a picture, explain a point to a peer, read out a unit of material to the class, make a correction without the teacher stepping in provide the meaning of a vocabulary item or a technical word, construct a sentence for the class, provide an example with the teacher's help and a whole lot of other things.

Each of the above aspects is an international act meant for the whole class to take benefit from. These and other acts that may crop up by the students' own initiative or initiated by the teacher can be manipulated and guided for the interactional benefit of the whole class. A sentence properly constructed by a student in a second language classroom is an asset that needs to be utilised by the teacher to provide language exposure to the whole class. The three sub-groups mentioned above should be dealt with differently in their initiation of and involvement in interactional situations. With different degrees of encouragement and with carefully provided feedback elements the teacher can involve all the three sub-groups into various interactional situations. The teacher should move but of the traditional pattern and restrictions of the classroom within the permitted framework and tap the potential of interactional situations that can be created in the classroom.

6. Developing Interaction-based Teaching Materials

Is it possible to develop interaction-based teaching materials? It would be interesting to examine this question in the light of all that we have seen about the nature and significance of classroom interaction. Teaching materials play a major role in effective teaching practices since these materials have a multidimensional function to perform as the material on which teachers and students alike depend for learning. The nature and quality of the teaching material considerably affect the learning process and the achievement however creative and resourceful the teacher may be. The dependence of the students on the textbook and other materials is considerable.

Any instructional (teaching) material can be said to be interaction-based if the quality and texture of the material can bring about optimum desired interaction in the learning situation, without the teacher needing to make special attempts for interaction. In other words interaction-based teaching materials should have the inherent structure (the format) for creating classroom interaction. A dialogue worked out for the purpose of dramatisation automatically brings about interaction since it contains as its automatically brings about interaction since it contains as its inherent structure an interactional situations. Here the teacher has only to permit the actual dramatisation of the dialogue . Hence a dialogue will be called an interaction-based instructional material.

A narrative or a descriptive passage with a set of questions at the end has the necessary interactional quality. Such a passage can by itself generate a question-answer session or a regular discussion especially if placed before a group for group work. Similarly, an inventory of question prepared by the teacher can generate the same activity during group work without the teacher needing to create an interactional situation. A language game worked out on paper in detail can generate classroom interaction in a regular class or in groups. All such materials are capable of functioning as interactional situations consisting of several interactional acts which the students will perform. While preparing teaching materials , then priority may be given to those formats which lend themselves easily to interactional situations. If the format cannot be moulded accordingly, then cues may be provided so that the teacher can easily convert those materials into clear interactional situations. An intelligent synthesis of classroom techniques and teaching materials with the teacher's own creative bent of mind can easily transform our classroom practices into highly interactional situations of a very fruitful kind.

8

GLOBAL TECHNIQUES FOR THE TEACHER

1. Nature of Global Techniques

A theory in philosophy, sociology, psychology, linguistics or education provides to the teacher directions in regard to the practices he should assume in providing classroom experiences to the learner. All theories and approaches to the classroom practice assume concreteness in the hands of the teacher only when he employs a specific act at a given instance to put cross a unit of information or to provide practice in a skill. By a classroom technique we exactly mean this act. A technique falls within the systemic framework of a method or overall procedure, proximately controlled by a specific approach to classroom teaching and is remotely controlled by a theory as indicated above.

A Technique as a specific and well-defined act, device or stimulus, employed by the teacher to initiate some form of classroom activity, falls under two categories: (a) classroom techniques of a global nature, and (b) classroom techniques of a specific nature. The first group consists of techniques such as questioning, and the second consists of techniques such as drill. Questioning is a global technique while drill is a highly language-specific technique. Global techniques with a totally pervasive nature as relevant to all language-specific and content-specific classrooms with great potential for classroom interaction. There are techniques like drill which is so language - specific that it has hardly any relevance in non-language classrooms.

A technique is a specific act, a device or stimulus that the teacher employs in the classroom. From the moment he enters the class-room until he leaves it the teacher does activities in general and acts in particular that are both definable and undefinable. By undefinable acts we mean any pattern or unit of behaviour that has nothing at all to do with the overall objective of a particular lesson. Under this category can come acts like a smile, scratching of one's head, a casual raising of one's hand, a variety of facial expressions, pacing in the classroom etc., which are so casual by nature that they do not in any way contribute to the overall objective of the particular lesson. We therefore do not label these as techniques in a technical sense of the term.

Classroom techniques are well-defined acts by the teacher having a definite direction defined with reference to the overall objective of the lesson in general, and to the specific objective of the step of a lesson in particular. A sketch that the teacher draws on the chalkboard, or sentence that he speaks out to the class are acts of the kind described above that we call classroom techniques. The teacher should be in a position to differentiate well these two kinds of acts in the classroom and achieve effective organisation of classroom techniques within the framework of an acceptable methodology.

Global techniques are those well-defined classroom acts of a pervasive nature which more or less constitute inherent components of teaching by its very nature and are therefore constituents of language - specific and content-specific teaching.

The most outstanding global techniques are : 1. Questioning, 2. Narration, 3. Demonstration and 4. Illustration. These four global techniques have such a pervasive nature that all kinds of classrooms employ these and these have become the backbone of classroom teaching. The teacher of English have to use these techniques both for providing information on aspects of English language as well as for developing in the students the various skills of English language. A teacher of chemistry uses the same techniques to put across a unit of information in the class as well as to consolidate and revise the student's learning of the particular unit.

The global techniques therefore have two dimensions: (a) A language-specific dimension that enables the language teacher to tap the resources of these techniques, and (b) a content-specific dimension that enables the subject teacher to tap the resources of such techniques for teaching content-matter. The teacher who belongs to either of these areas uses these techniques to create interactional and communicative situations and through the involvement of students in a variety of ways teach the unit in an effective manner.

The global techniques have great potential for classroom teaching and the teacher depends on these with considerable frequency. The chief reason for these is that these techniques as classroom practices are *multidimensional* by nature, in the sense that these techniques can be applied differently in different teaching situations and for different teaching units, and within the teaching units for different steps in the teaching of the same lesson. Questioning for instance is so comprehensive and pervasive that there is hardly any teaching unit, teaching step or situation to which this technique cannot be applied in one form or other. Illustration, similarly is so global in its structure that a large variety of practices emanate from this single technique. The same is true of narration and demonstration which have great and comprehensive potential as classroom techniques.

2. Questioning as a Global Techniques

Questioning is the most dominant of global techniques with an exceptionally pervasive character. Questioning has been understood and accepted as a device of classroom teaching from time immemorial with a large variety of functions attached to it. Different fields of studies have viewed questioning from very different perspectives. Philology views the process of questioning as a literary device, which goes into the making of a written discourse. The present - day discourse analysis has taken up this issue as part of the study of stylistics and looks into the process of questioning as a stylistic device for discourse construction. Stress is put on the structural aspects of questions as a language element in the development of writing and discourse analysts view it from a variety of structural perspectives such as : 1. How do questions link the stages in the development of a discourse unit such as a dialogue? 2. What are the logical functions of a question ? 3. How does a question function as a literary device in a piece of literature ? Into how many structural categories can questions be divided? and so on. Under this scheme of analysis the structure and function of questions are often viewed chiefly from the mental process that is involved in processing the answers. What type of a mental process is involved when the student attempts an answer to this question ?

Under such a scheme as this whose origins can be traced back to philology and has been widely accepted in educational circles, questions are classified as: 1. factual questions, 2. analysis questions, 3. explanatory questions, 4. critical questions, 5. judgement questions and so on. These terms are related to the mental process that the student employs in his attempts to find an answer. While question papers are set for examinations these have often been thought of as the criteria to follow. All this is just one view point from which to analyse the nature of what we know as questions and questioning. This helps us recognise the role questions as a factor in the use of language has played in the history of human knowledge in general and education in particular.

While the term 'question' implies a structural approach with specific reference to *a form of construction* either asked in communicative context or written down for a purpose. In formal grammar this form of construction is known as interrogative construction. Every language has a formal pattern to express this construction. As a universal phenomenon this linguistic construction or linguistic function can be done either through the formal interrogative pattern or through the use of an alteration in intonation as in:

1. Are they all going to leave the place ?
2. They are all going to leave the place (?)

In the first sentence there is an inversion involved to make the construction specifically interrogative; in the latter sentence an affirmative statement is used to carry out the same function coupled with an intonation proper to an interrogative sentence. The first is part of the standard, formal language; the second is acceptable only in colloginal (informal) usage.

English language teaching has employed the term '*questioning*' to mean not the interrogative construction as a structural element, but the process of employing such a construction as a teaching technique. The technique therefore is not the question, but the act of questioning. This distinction at the teacher's level can create an added consciousness of the role this technique plays in classroom teaching. Questioning as a technique is an act that the teacher employs in the context of teaching *to evoke a response* on the part of the learner to condition a specific form of behaviour. This behaviour may be the comprehension of a sentence in the language, consolidation of proficiency in the use of information that the teacher has already put across. The teacher employs this technique for a variety of purposes as we shall examine later.

Questioning as a technique is primarily *language-specific*. The teaching of speech, grammar, vocabulary, reading, composition and poetry employs the technique of questioning as a unique interactional act or stimulus. In every one of these lessons as we shall see in detail in the following pages the technique of questioning is used with one interactional specification or other, as part of one teaching step or other. Every time questioning is used at a given step of teaching the purpose considerably varies. This purpose we shall define in the present context as the functions of questioning. On the basis of these functions we shall divide the technique of questioning into four major categories. These categories of questioning though functional by nature as a technique will be expressed structurally as questions with reference to the *content of questioning* in all the four categories. The four categories are :

1. Lead Questions.
2. Reflective Questions.
3. Analytic Questions.
4. Evaluative Questions.

In language-specific as well as content-specific classrooms the four categories become relevant and functional. All the same language classrooms make more elaborate use of these categories of questions to carryout language functions and to make communicative use of language as well as to achieve interaction.

3. The Role of Lead Questions in Teaching

The four categories of questions mentioned above constitute the methodological way of grouping questioning in classroom teaching. The grouping is done not on the basis of the kind of mental process that will go on into the processing of answers by students but the grouping of questioning (questions) is done on the basis of the *methodological function* questioning has at every step in the teaching of specific lessons. *Lead questions* are the kind of questions which are employed as a technique to lead students to the theme of the topic in a variety of lessons.

Reflective questions are the kind of questions that are employed as a technique in the form of an illustrative aid in a variety of situations in teaching. No answer is expected to these questions. These are used just as an illustrative aid mostly during presentation. *Analytic questions* are the kind of questions which are employed as a technique to help students exercise their minds deeper into the theme of a topic in an analytic manner in the form of a discussion. All questions meant to initiate a discussion fall under this category.

Evaluative questions are the kind of questions that are employed as a technique to test the achievement of the class either as part of a regular lesson or as an achievement test.

Lead questions have a major role to play in the teaching of English at all levels. The term 'lead' signifies the specific function of linking the new with the known. All lessons whether language lessons or subject lessons aim at teaching a new unit of information. This new unit has an internal structure of its own together with its content-matter to put across. Ordinarily it will be methodologically illogical to begin teaching the elements of the new unit without relating it to some area that students are familiar with. This may be in the form of a revision of the material previously taught, the material that logically precedes the new unit as in the case of grammar items, or of the material that falls within the learner's sphere of experience as in the case of a composition lesson. Lead questions occur in the following areas:

1. *A Grammar Lesson* has lead questions as its initial work. Initial work is any form of preliminary activity that the teacher undertakes before the presentation of the new unit. Out of a number of different techniques that the teacher may use for initial work questioning is just one, but the most potential one. The content of a grammar lesson will be either a formal aspect of grammar or a structural item. The lead questions will be a set of questions whose function is to lead the students to the new aspect of grammar. The questions are called lead questions only if there is thematic relation between the presentation work and the initial work. The questions will evoke answers from students, which contain material taught previously.

2. *A Vocabulary Lesson* has lead questions as its Initial Work. A vocabulary lesson has as its content-matter a set of new vocabulary items taken from a unit of the lesson in the text-book. The new items will be

taught using a discourse unit (a paragraph) in which the vocabulary items are carefully used. This discourse has naturally a theme. The teacher himself works out this discourse. The teacher then chooses four or five questions that will be used as the technique at the Initial Work to lead the students to the theme of the discourse used in the Presentation. These questions and the Presentation work are thematically connected. The questions do the function of linking the new theme and a theme that is proximate, easier, known to the class better. If the discourse is worked out on a theme like the zoo, then the lead questions can be on animals with which the class is most familiar.

3. *A Reading Lesson* employs lead questions as its Initial Work. The lesson may be an intensive reading lesson or an extensive reading lesson. The former provides training in careful, detailed and analytic reading of study materials; while the latter provides training in general, faster and non-detailed reading, In both the cases the lesson is based on a unit of lesson in the text-book, the first part, the second part or the third part. Questions constitute the Initial Work of a reading lesson. In both the kind of lessons the Initial Work is the same i.e., to lead the students to the theme of the discourse unit the class will be reading. If the reading is done on the first part of the lesson in the text, the lead questions will be based on a theme related to the lesson. It will be a transition from a simpler topic to the theme of the lesson. If reading is done on the second or the last part of the lesson, the lead questions will be revision questions drawn from the preceding part of the textbook lesson.

4. *A Composition Lesson and A Poetry Lesson* have lead questions as their Initial Work. A composition has a theme as its content; the same is true of poetry. The presentation of the poem and the development of the composition are centred on the thematic aspects on which these are based. The teacher selects a set of questions on a simpler, proximate and related topic and uses these as lead questions during the Initial Work. The function, again, is to establish a link between a topic they are familiar with the theme of the poem or of the composition. In all the above cases questions are not meant for deeper understanding, initiate thinking or for evaluating the students' achievement.

4. The Role of Reflective Questions in Teaching

The present work envisages two major groups of questions; (a) genuine questions and (b) reflective questions. Of the category of four mentioned above, 1, 3 and 4 are genuine questions which expect an answer from the listener/reader. But reflective questions are conceived of as what has traditionally been called *rhetoric questions.* Reflective questions are rhetoric questions which constitute a significant part of all forms of teaching, especially of lecture method, talks or any forms of teaching, especially of lecture method, talks or any form of narration. The term 'reflective' indicates that the questioning is done as a *rhetoric device* to spark off a degree of thinking in the listeners. As a technique reflective questions aim at the following : 1. the speaker employs such questions as the talk is in progress with a view to making them think on the points that he is making. 2. Reflective questions are employed to create among the audience an awareness of the seriousness of a point that the speaker is making. This is done by attracting their attention through a question that is carefully formulated with greater appeal. 3. Reflective questions are employed, again as a rhetoric device to establish a link between two important points in the talk. The question remains sandwiched between the two points and the audience will then easily see the link that exists between a point that the speaker has made and the one he is going to make. The following areas of second language teaching can employ reflective questions as part of the regular lessons:

1. *The teaching of formal grammar* makes use of reflective questions at the time the teacher presents the formal aspects of, say, the tenses of English. A question such as: 'What is the different between the present progressive tense and the simple present tense?' or 'How does the simple present tense express habitual actions?' During the Presentation of the formal aspects of the tenses the teacher asks these questions not for the class to provide an answer but to make them think on the one hand, and specify for them the area with which the teacher is dealing. He does not expect an answer or wait for the students to provide an answer because that precisely is the aspect that he is going to teach. Such reflective questions used on numerous occasions function as a rhetoric technique to create among the students an awareness of the exact point he is dealing with.

2. *The teaching of functional grammar* employs reflective questions during the Presentation of the structural item or a sentence pattern. There arises a number of occasions when the teacher has to pose well-framed questions before the class. The teaching point, for instance, is simple

present tense, and the teacher at the time of Presentation asks: which place does Sunil's father visit in summer?' He does not point to the class for an answer. Instead he employs the teaching point in the answer-construction and says: 'Sunil's father visits Kashmir in Summer.' His aim is to *make the class understand* the meaning and a specific use of the simple present tense. For this he requires a suitable sentence. The best way to obtain such a sentence for him is to pause a question. The class links easily the question and the answer and thereby understands the usage.

3. *The teaching of Interrogative Patterns* of all types in functional grammar employs reflective questions as a Presentation technique. Since the teaching item itself is a question pattern the teacher speaks aloud a sentence: 'Sunil's father visits Kashmir in Summer'. The teaching point is the question pattern of this sentence and he uses the above declarative pattern as his starting point. Then he says: 'Which place does Sunil's father visit in summer?' or 'Which place lies to the south of Gujarat?' The teacher is using these questions as part of his *Verbal illustration* and no answer from the students is expected. In fact he often begins with the answer itself before he clearly speaks out the question, and writes the question on the chalkboard without the answer to give a greater focus to the new pattern.

4. *The teaching of vocabulary* employs reflective questions at the time of Presentation when the new vocabulary at the time of Presentation when the new vocabulary items are introduced. Questioning has no other function to perform at this step. The teacher uses a variety of demonstrative and illustrative techniques to carry home the meaning and use of the new words. But after illustrating every word he asks a question or two of a reflective kind just to acquaint the class with the way the new word can be used in a question. If the teacher obtains the answer, then it is only for the sake of classroom interaction.

5. *Reflective Questions in Content-specific teaching*: Reflective questions are an intrinsic part of narrative, lecture-like teaching where the pupils have no definite involvement. The teacher stops at certain points and poses a question. The purpose is rhetoric; this gives a break to the continuity of the talk or narration (see Mono. No. 1), gives the students an occasion to think; and it functions as a stimulus for them to pay closer attention. Reflective questions can be effectively knit into the sequential structure of the narration as a discourse. Even when

students are given opportunities to join in it is done so for the sake of enhancing classroom interaction. Reflective questions thus play a major role in narrative (lecture) form of teaching.

5. The Role of Analytic Questions in Teaching

If lead questions have the function of leading to a theme, reflective questions have a rhetoric function, then analytic questions aim at helping the students exercise their minds in obtaining a *deeper understanding* of the material the class is working on. Questions here function as a device for the teacher to indicate to the class the areas of significance in a discourse material. Questions are framed in such a way that they are once reflect those points in the discourse which the class should focus on. Questions are asked either on materials that the class may have just read, or listened to, or on materials with which the class is ordinarily familiarly. In all such instances the teacher employs the technique of questioning to help the class delve deeper in an analytic manner into the theme of the discourse unit. Analytic questions are global by nature and are used by both language-specific and content-specific teaching. The following areas of teaching employs analytic questions as a classroom technique.

1. *The teaching of grammar* employs analytic questions when the teacher attempts to give Meaningful/Communicative practice. This is the step after the pupils have understood the meaning and use of the grammatical structure and undertaken Drill work using the structure. The teacher's aim during the meaningful / communicative practice is to help the class use the structure in meaningful/communicative contexts. The teacher asks a sequence of analytic questions which make the class think, analyse the situation on which the questions are based, and if possible discuss a few things in the form of question-answers. Deeper understanding of the use of the structure and greater practice in the use of the structure result from analytic questions.

2. *The teaching of vocabulary* employs analytic questions at the Meaningful/Communicative practice step, as in the case of teaching grammar. After the vocabulary is introduced to the class using a variety of adequate techniques the teacher can provide practice using a few selected sentences to acquaint the class with the formal usage of each new word introduced during the Presentation. Once this is done the teacher can resort to the use of questioning to initiate communicative

use of the words in the class. These questions are analytic by nature, and aim at providing the class a deeper understanding of the meaning of the vocabulary items and greater practice in their use.

3. *The Teaching of Reading* (intensive and extensive reading) has analytic questioning as the most important technique at the step of Discussion. Analytic questioning shows out its optimum potential as a technique in the teaching of reading, composition and poetry. In an intensive reading lesson the teacher provides a model reading and supervises the students' silent reading; in an extensive reading class the teacher supervises the silent reading session without the teacher's reading. After the reading is conducted well, the teacher employs the technique of analytic questioning. He asks very detailed, analytic questions taking into consideration all the important points in the intensive reading discourse. The questioning is not meant as lead questions, reflective questions or evaluation questions, but as analytic questions. The purpose is purely to help students obtain a deeper comprehension of the contents of the passage, and to have language practice through the high level interaction possible at this step.

4. *The Teaching of Composition* employs analytic questioning as the technique for developing in detail the points of the discourse meant to be constructed by individual students either orally or in writing. After asking the lead questions at the Initial Work the teacher employs a sequentially organised set of questions for the development of the points. These questions are purely analytic by nature. The purpose is to create interaction, help students think analytically and in a logical manner, link the patterns of interrogation used by the teacher and of declaration by the students in terms of the structural specifications, and practice the listening - speaking skill using a definite set of grammatical structures and vocabulary items. The questions are very detailed in intensive reading lessons, while they are more general in extensive reading lessons.

5. *The Teaching of Poetry* uses analytic questions, similarly, in the Discussion step. The poems is recited by the teacher, and then by a few students to help the class *listen* to it several times. Then the teacher uses analytic questions to initiate discussion. Poetry is taught for appreciation of the aesthetic use of language. A knowledge of the content of the poem is a means to this objective. Poetry teaching in schools is never information-oriented. At the discussion stage the teacher asks analytic questions at two levels: (a) to help the pupils know the

sound scheme of the poem, and (b) to help them know the thematic content of the poem. This analysis helps them appreciate the poem to a much greater extent.

6. *Consolidation of Content-specific Units :* In the teaching of content-specific subjects like geography, analytic questioning has a major role to play. The teacher presents the unit using any of the techniques recommended for a subject like geography. Then he employs a sequence of analytic questions to consolidate the students' knowledge of the unit taught. As in the case the reading lesson discussed above, the teacher resorts to the technique recommended for a subject like geography. Then he employs a sequence of analytic questions to consolidate the students' knowledge of the unit taught. As in the case the reading lesson discussed above, the teacher resorts to the technique of analytic questioning and helps the class 1. understand the content matter better, 2. express themselves using the information in an organised manner, 3. familiarise themselves better with technical language that occurs in the material, and 4. revise the material in a more detailed manner. In all such instances as described above analytic questions are employed by the teacher as a unique technique capable of creating most productive interaction in the class.

6. The Role of Evaluative Questions in Teaching

Evaluate questions unlike the categories discussed above, have the function of *measuring the achievement* of the students of particular level in any particular area of learning. The term evaluation signifies the role these questions have in the classroom. Testing and measurement with reference to education have the specific function of evaluation for any given purpose: (a) to know the level achievement as an aid to teaching, (b) to know the level of achievement for research purposes, (c) to promote the class to a higher level. Two types of *test material* are made use of which contain what I shall call *test techniques.* A test technique indicates the process (mental process) that is involved in processing the answers. A *question* is a test technique or *blank filling* in an objective test is also Test Technique. It is the specific device teacher uses for measuring the student's performance. We shall recognise three types of *test formats* in evaluation and measurement. They are: 1. Essay type, 2. short answer type, and 3. objective type. These are test formats for evaluation using a variety of test techniques that consists of *test items* on which students work.

The present concern is not with (b) or (c) above, but only with (a) i.e., to know how far the class has learned a teaching unit. Evaluative questions we are concerned about in the present context are a constituent of the teaching methodology the teacher is employing for a particular unit. The evaluation is meant for measuring the achievement of the class with reference to his own not only the achievement of the class but also the success of the teacher's own work in the class. The following areas make use of evaluative questions:

1. *Evaluative questions* are employed when the teacher arranges *an oral test* to find out the achievement of the class. The answers the students give are not corrected or got repeated by other students because the aim is not practice or discussion. 2. Evaluative questions are employed by the teacher as part of a written test that he may administer from time to time to measure for himself the student's performance.

2. *A grammar lesson* may use evaluative questions as the last step in the teaching of a grammar. After having presented the material and having meaningful/communicative practice the teacher may use a set of evaluative questions to find out how far the material has been learned by the class. No corrections and no repetition of answers need to be involved in this particular technique. These should as far as possible be directed to the average and slow learner group of the class.

3. *A vocabulary lesson* can have evaluative questions, again, as the last step. After introducing the new words, and providing practice of the kinds mentioned above the teacher employs evaluative questions of a definite kind to find out to what extent the class has learned the meaning and use of the new vocabulary items. The short and precise answers the students give will show if they have really understood the meaning of the words. Focus should not be put on the overall structure of the answer but only on the use of the word. In all these cases we have traditionally recommended the use of objective type formats. The teacher is free to choose either or drop this step all together if he doesn't feel the need for it.

4. *A reading lesson* can use evaluative questioning as a technique after the discussion on the content matter of the passage is over. The teacher can try out the feasibility of using regular questions for finding out to what extent the class as a whole and individuals in particular have

comprehended the material of the lesson. The students will answer these few questions without the use of the textbook and without the step by step help of the teacher as it happens in all other forms of questioning.

5. *A poetry lesson* may have evaluative questioning as the final step in the teaching especially at higher levels. At higher levels we give greater importance to the thematic content of the poem. After the regular recitation, discussion and final group recitation of the poem the teacher will use a few selected questions to find out if they have really understood the thematic aspects and the sound scheme of the poem. At higher levels greater premium is placed on the thematic content and hence the evaluative questions too will have greater stress on content-specific questions. Evaluative questions thus help the teacher judge the achievement of the class as well as the adequacy of the techniques he has used.

7. The Global Technique of Narration

Just as questioning as a technique of classroom teaching penetrates all aspects of teaching, narration functions as a global technique in all aspects of both language - specific and content—specific teaching. We are not using the term narration in its very narrow sense of speaking out a discourse pertaining to a past event using any form of the past tense, as contrasted to description. *Narration* is used in the context of English language teaching as any form of *exposition* used as a classroom technique to present to the class a quantum of information pertaining a theory or practice. Narration thus is any expository talk (see Mono. 1) given by the teacher for a considerable length of time i.e., as a short or lengthy discourse (oral).

In other words narration is an *oral discourse* since it is conceived of as a classroom technique, which has the cohesion and coherence of a linguistic discourse unit, to convey a quantum of information to the class. When narration is the principal technique that governs a full class hour without sizeable break employing interactional techniques such a narration is called *a lecture.* It is narrative or expository techniques that go into the making of a lecture that is characteristic of college and university teaching. Narration as an expository techniques is basically without interactional potentials but there are definite ways of transforming the narrative technique into an active, interaction -oriented activity (see Mono. No.1 for details). The following areas of teaching employ narration for classroom teaching:

1. *Content-specific teaching* employs narration quite elaborately. A well-prepared teacher of geography, for instance, will enter the class, do the Initial Work, and then do the Presentation of the teaching unit using the technique of narration. He exposes the material to the class in the form of a talk before he switches over to any other activity of demonstration, questioning or group work by students. Narration becomes the very centre of content - specific teaching to put across information regarding a theory or a practice.

2. Narration is employed in teaching *spoken English*. The teaching of spoken English has specific-aspects like conversational English as its content. The teacher may use the narration of a short discourse at the Presentation step as the basis for the teacher's work on pronunciation, spoken English or conversational aspects. Narration provides the class with an opportunity to quietly listen to the teaching unit knit into the discourse which the teacher is narrating.

3. Narration is used in the teaching of *formal grammar*. *Formal grammar* takes care of the students' knowledge about the formal aspects of English grammar. The teacher resorts to the technique of narration to provide explanation about the nature and function of an aspect of grammar such as the articles in English. Narration serves the purpose here since the aim is to *provide* information regarding the formal aspect of grammar.

4. Narration has a significant place as a technique in teaching *vocabulary*. The new words are to be presented in an adequate discourse context, may be a story or a paragraph. After the Initial Work the teacher begins the narration of the discourse with or without the help of any written material. It is from this story or paragraph that the teacher takes out the vocabulary items one by one and introduces the item using an adequate technique.

5. *Teaching Composition using a story* employs narration at the first part of the Discourse Building step. The teacher narrates the story in English at the outset, then develops the story again through a question - answer session; the same story is constructed by the individual student either orally or in writing. *A poetry lesson* too may use narration at the step of Initial Work. The narration of a short event or story can substitute

the lead questions (3:4) as the preliminary work in the teaching of poetry.

8. The Global Technique of Illustration

Illustrative techniques as this group has often been called are for the purpose of theoretical convenience brought together under the global term *Illustration.* Illustrative technique are employed by the teacher either in language-specific or content-specific teaching to bring home to the class *the meaning of a teaching unit.* The term 'meaning' here stands for 'the form, meaning and use' of a language item in language teaching or the content-specifications of a given unit in content-specific teaching. In all these cases the teacher's aim is to pass on to the class (*make the class understand*) what exactly the form, meaning and use of a language item is, or what exactly a content-specification is. The teacher at this stage does not aim at any revision, or any practice, or any form of evaluation. He just wants the class to understand a few things. Illustrative techniques serve exactly this purpose.

What do we mean by illustrative techniques? Illustrative techniques fall under three categories: 1. *Demonstrative Illustration*, 2. *Pictorial Illustration*, and 3. *Verbal Illustration*. Demonstrative illustration is the technique of teaching the meaning of a unit through the use of : (a) actions, (b) objects, and (c) experiments (in laboratory situations). The teacher attempts to teach the class the meaning of the unit using any of these devices which involves demonstration. Demonstration is employed as the vehicle for the illustration of the specific meaning of the unit. Hence we have called it demonstrative illustration.

Pictorial illustration is the technique of using the visual representation (modality) of a picture, diagram, sketch or chart to teach the meaning of a given unit of language or content. A major distinction to be aware of by the teacher is that all uses of picture in the classroom are not pictorial illustration. A picture may be used in a variety of situations merely as a *teaching aid.* At the Initial Work step of a grammar lesson if the teacher uses a picture he is not employing the technique of pictorial illustration, but merely using the picture or action as an aid to the actual use of the unit of language which is in fact only a revision. The same is true when a composition is taught using a picture. The process does not involve pictorial illustration; the picture is merely used as an aid and a basis for the class to work out the points for the composition. There is no illustration taking place at this context. This is an important distinction to bear in mind.

Verbal illustration is the technique of using verbal modality (language itself) to teach the meaning of a given unit of language or content. Instead of using a picture, on object or an action, here the teacher employs language itself to illustrate the meaning. Hence the term verbal illustration. The work consists in the creation of a verbal context, communicative context or a situation and sentence are constructed based on the situation. Verbal illustration becomes necessary in the case of functional grammar on the one hand and abstract vocabulary items on the other. It is the use of adequate examples rather than explanation of the structure or vocabulary items.

Illustration of all kinds are employed at the Presentation step of teaching *grammar* and *vocabulary* to bring home the meaning of the item. The sentences that the teacher speaks out at the Presentation of a grammar item constitutes verbal illustration because the sentences have an illustrative function to perform. Pictorial illustration and demonstrative illustration are more used in the teaching of vocabulary. If a picture shows an action that indicates a grammatical structure and if it is used for teaching that meaning the technique will be called pictorial illustration. Content-specific teaching employs more demonstrative illustration and pictorial illustration than verbal illustration. Illustrative techniques thus play a major role in both language - specific and content-specific teaching. The creative and resourceful teacher should develop an awareness of the potential of these global techniques and make his classroom teaching a pleasant and fruitful experience.

9

DESIGN AND USE OF LOW-COST AIDS

1. The Role of Instructional Aids in the Classroom

The teacher in the classroom has at his disposal a large variety of factors to organise as part of his classroom teaching as a system to undertake effective teaching. The interaction that he is expected to undertake effective teaching. The interaction that he is expected to achieve between the students and himself depends on the nature of this organisation of the teaching components. Broadly speaking he has four different components at his disposal :1. *the language* which functions as the medium, 2.the content material that is to be put across, 3.the classroom techniques which he employs , and 4.the *teaching materials* which are at his creative resources to coordinate these components of the system in such a way that his work emerges as most productive.

Teaching or instructional materials as these have often been called, provide the basis, the starting point, and the points of reference for the students, and the teacher's teaching-learning activities in the classroom. These teaching materials consist of (a)*language materials* and (b)instructional aids. Language materials that the teacher depends on consists of the textbook and other non-detailed, supplementary books, prescribed as part of the official syllabus . *Instructional (teaching) aids* are all those materials that the teacher brings into the classroom from time to time to facilitate his teaching and to make the work more creative and effective. These are generally known as teaching aids. Each of these functions as a component of the overall system of classroom teaching.

Instruction aids that help the teacher as resourceful devices in his classroom practices can be conveniently grouped under the following categories: 1.*Visual aids*, 2.*Audio-model aids*,and 3.*Audio-Visual aids*. Visual aids are those instructional aids which functions through their visual modality in providing the instructional stimuli. Audio-modal aids are those instructional aids that function through their auditory stimuli. And audio-visual aids provides the instructional stimuli through both visual and auditory modalities. These three components of the sub-system of instructional aids have the full coverage of whatever materials the teacher may introduce into the class from time to time.

The following may be considered the role that instructional aids play in classroom teaching :

(a) instructional aids help the teacher add a new and concrete dimension to classroom teaching .His dependence on the materials in the text-book and supplementary books can easily lead to stereotyped mode of teaching. Introducing aids to the classroom helps him add a new dimension to his teaching.

(b) Instructional aids make language teaching a practical affair having brought down the abstract categories of language to perceptible reality in the classroom. The teaching of formal grammar as well as of functional grammar can be made a down-to earth affair by the use of instructional aids.

(c) Instructional aids help content-specific teaching have orientations and directions that would otherwise tax the imagination of students while assimilating the content-matter of a particular unit. A geography or a science classroom depends on instructional aids by the very nature of those disciplines and they require demonstrative illustrations.

(d) Instructional aids function as the primary tool for classroom interaction. The teacher who aims at creative classroom interaction cannot afford to neglect the use of instructional aids as a means to creating interaction, both peer-interaction and student-teacher interaction. Instructional materials may be commercially available or needs to be prepared by the teacher himself. In school situations a conscientious teacher will be able to develop a conviction with regard to the usefulness of instructional aids of a feasible kind and be on the look out for aids that are quite handy for his apt use in teaching situations.

2. The Nature of Visual Aids for the Classroom

Visual aids are those instructional aids that function through their visual modality in providing instructional stimuli. The classroom naturally depends primarily on the visual and arbitory potentials of the learners for all the work that takes place there. Visual modality is a sense medium that the teacher exploits to pass on to the class units of information, to develop a variety of skills in the learners, and bring about desirable behaviour changes of a variety of kinds . The following visual aids constitute the basic material for the teacher to provide the necessary instructional stimuli for adequate learning to take place in the class :

The Chalkboard as a Visual Aid: The chalkboard is the most handy, readily available and all purpose visual aid for the teacher's use in the classroom. It offers great scope as the simplest aid that the teacher can make creative use of . The following can be the area where the chalkboard can best be used:

(a) *The teaching of content-specific lessons* offers considerable scope for the use of the chalkboard. The teacher makes creative use of this aid in presenting sketches diagrams, outlines, schematic presentation of a unit, presentation of technical vocabulary, outline of a unit for revision and so on.

(b) *The teaching of functional grammar* can be made effective by the use of the chalkboard during presentation, Drill and Communicative practice. Typical sentences for Presentation, Substitution tables or patterns for Drill and Sketches, figures, for and outlines for communicative practice will be the visual material for which the chalkboard will be used.

(c) *The teaching of vocabulary* can be made effective by the use of the chalkboard during Presentation, and Communicative practice. Typical sentences using the words during presentation, sketches and drawings for pictorial illustration of the vocabulary items, and a variety of base materials for communicative activities can all be part of the use of the chalkboard.

(d) *The teaching of Composition* can be made effective by the use of the chalkboard during the development of the composition frame. Step by step the frame for the oral or written composition can be developed of the chalkboard on the basis of which the student will construct the whole discourse.

Apart from these the chalkboard becomes handy in teaching poetry for the presentation of *drawings* at the Initial Work, in teaching poetry for the presentation of minimal pairs at Presentation and Practice, in teaching Graphics for the Presentation of model letters and writing, and in teaching rules. The teacher has only to exercise his mind to make the right use of the chalkboard .

The chalkboard is given priority in the present context as the best and most readily available visual aid. Any teacher at any level and in the teaching with reference to his mind in regard to the use of the chalkboard. See Monograph 1 , for details as to how the chalkboard be best used as part of regular lectures .

Other important visual aids we shall examine later with regard to their use are: 1. *pictures* of various kinds, 2. *charts* prepared for specific uses, 3. *flannel board* on which creative material can be put up, 4. magnetboard that can substitute the chalkboard but has more elaborate uses, 5. *flash cards* handy for the teacher to use in the classroom, 6. *flashboards* to be placed in class, 7.*flashcard* stands on which the flashcards can be arranged, 8. *picture cards* which can be used in a variety of teaching situations 9. *puzzle cards* that can present language material from which sentences can be framed in the form of puzzles, 10. *actral objects* to be used for purposes of demonstration, 11. *slides* as a technological aid accessible to the teacher, 12. *an overhead projector* to be used for a variety of interactional situations , 13. *an opaque projector* which can project actual pictures and pages of the textbook or other material, 14. *film strips* that can introduce language situations in the classroom and 15. *models* of various kinds that can go with content-specific teaching.

The manifold instructional aids grouped above have one and the same fundamental function to do . Every one of these visual aids functions as instructional material through their visual modality. It will be noticed that every one of these aids constitutes a base material on which or through which language material or content-matter is presented. Hence we have two dimensions of all these aids: 1. *the software material* and 2. *the hardware material* which are commonly known as the hardware and the software. This distinction is especially true of technological devices such as the overhead projector , language laboratory or the video. The machines constitute the hardware which function as the tools for the presentation of the software which consists of the actual language or content matter for the students to learn. The visual language or content matter for the students to learn. The visual aids that have been enumerated above constitute a creative and productive resource which both in language-specific and content-specific teaching situations the teacher can produce and employing a variety of ways specifically attached to steps and points of teaching.

3. The Role of Audio-modal Aids for the Classroom

Audio-modal aids are those instructional aids which functional through their auditory modality in providing the instructional stimuli necessary for the teacher's classroom practices. The classroom activities, in their fundamentals, are audio-modal by nature since even if no aid is made use of the teacher himself speaks using one technique or the other, and creates an audio-modal (often called audio-lingual)atmosphere. In most cases the class sees nothing except the teacher's work on the chalkboard, or perhaps in several cases of classroom teaching no use of the chalkboard is made and the learning-stimuli in the class remain purely audio-modal. Audio-modal aids when the teacher uses them provides auditory or listening experience. The record-player is an obvious example. The teaching of both language-specific and content-specific lessons have opportunities to make use of audio-modal aids. But these have greater application to language teaching situation .

1. *The Radio :* The radio has been recognised as a most potential and resourceful audio-modal aid. Right from stray and casual educational programmes broadcast over the radio, to systems such as 'open universities' and 'distance education' the resourcefulness of the radio is made use of. The radio provides strictly audio-modal learning experiences and the teacher needs to have a scheme to guide the students with regard to the educational use of the radio. All India Radio for instance has regular State-wise programmes for the teaching of languages such as English and Hindi specially oriented to the needs of different levels of language teaching. The oriented to the needs of different levels of language teaching. The radio can be helpful to the teaching of English in the following manner:

(a) Programmes of specific directions should be *broadcast* from local stations during the working hours of schools in reasonable frequency so that these may be listened to by students guided by teachers. These programmes if found effective can become part of the curriculum.

(b) programmes with definite orientations should be *broadcast* either in a centralised manner or from local stations with as much content coverage as possible with less frequency to students or teachers of English certain important aspects of the language.

(c) teachers of English, for instance, *will record discourse units* in general such as news bulletins or talks , or programmes of a very specific nature from the radio. These recordings can then be presented to the class at convenient times constituting these presentations regular part of teaching. This becomes more relevant when the teacher desires to give the class a bulls-eye or a modal of the language for their pursual and study.

2. *Record-Player :* Another audio-visual technological aid is the tape-recorder the use of which for English language teaching cannot be overstressed. The language-laboratory which is so widely recognised as a very useful audio-lingual technological device is fundamentally a set of record-players with listening-speaking recording facilities. Leaving the utility of the language laboratory apart, teacher in the classroom has numerous ways of providing his class listening-recording-playback facilities in both language and content-specific teaching.

2. *Language-laboratory*: The language laboratory basically consists of cassette record-players that are organised in such a way that unified language work can be undertaken. With a master-panel to control and guide laboratory positions numerous dimensions of instructional and testing activities in listening comprehension and oral expression can be undertaken. The language laboratory equipment constitutes the hardware and the material that goes into the recording constitutes the software. It is possible for a school to organise the model of a mini-language laboratory and provide students listening-speaking practice. What is needed is adequate material for the work.

4. The Role of Audio-visual Devices in Teaching

Audio-visual devices are those instructional aids which function through both their auditory and visual modalities in providing the instructional stimuli necessary for the teacher's activities. There is controversy on whether the uni-model (unisensory) simuli or bimodal (multi-sensory) stimuli are more crucial and effective in classroom learning or for effective perception in general. In other words whether learning will better take place by intensive listening to a unimodal device like to radio or a bimodal device like the television. No experimental proof for the effectiveness of either has been available. Yet experience and observation tell us that intense listening to the radio enables our cognitive faculty to subsume a comprehensive and detailed quantum of information while over a bimodal presentation like the television we fluctuate every moment between the co-presentation of the auditory and visual stimuli. This fluctuation is a psychological phenomenon. Our attention is capable of subsuming only one stimulus at a time; we fluctuate between the stimuli in mullisenory situations.

Audio-visual devices on the other hand is found to be most effective not because of the combination of the two modalities but because of the presentation of visual modality in particular. The auditory presentation functions as an aid to the intake of the auditory stimuli. Audio-visual devices have been recognised and accepted as a fruitful manner of presenting educational material in general and language material in particular. These have been brought into the classroom and elaborate preparation is being done undertaken to reach every classroom in the country through INSAT-1-B. The following constitute what we have called audiovisual devices:

1. *The Television* : With the utilisation of satellites like the INSAT-1-B the potential of the television has become great. It is hoped that every classroom in the country will in the near future be able to exploit the instructional resources of the television. The installation of a grater number of television centres in the country to relay programmes telecast by the satellite will ensure in course of time the plans of the Government of India in this regard. The television like the radio can become both a curricular as well as a co-curricular component of education in general and English language teaching in particular. Educational programmes specifically geared to a particular level can become part of the regular curricular work if the telecast is made during the working hours and the programme is on the spot guided by the teacher and followed-up the class. Co-curricular programmes over the television can be of lower frequency and may not specifically be attached to the student's regular

syllabus and other materials.

2. *The Video*: The television has a number of limitations since it is some how or other centrally controlled like the radio. The video on the other hand can be at the disposal of individual schools and the teacher can have easy access to this facility. Every institution should have a television and video room like a Common Room. While educational television programmes should be attended by as many classes as such a room can contain, the video should be at the disposal of teachers for presenting programmes content-centres or language-specific material such as those available from the BBC, to the class geared to the specific needs of the syllabus.

3. *Films* : Films constitute another audiovisual technological device for teaching. Films are two kinds: *documentary films and feature films.* Educational and English language teaching films are available from the BBC through the British Council (Bombay, Delhi, Madras). These are based on very specific teaching material. The following titles include documentary films and video cassettes available from the BBC through the British Council in India:

BBC Television Video Productions:

1. Follow Me : 60 Units e.g., "Welcome to Britain."
2. On We go: 30 units e.g., "Mark is ill."
3. People you Meet: 26 units e.g., "I have forgotton it."
4. Challenges: 6 units e.g., "Somewhere to live."
5. The Sadrina Project: 12 units. e.g., "On Travel / Tourism."
6. The Bellcrest Story - 13 units e.g., Advance course for Business Transactions.
7. Songs Alive : 10 units: Based on Songs.
8. Comedy Time: 4 units: Based on Entertainment.
9. Teaching Observed: 13 units: Classes at work in 6 countries.
10. Follow Me to Sanfransisco : 10 units: People in the U.S.A.

The teacher of English should work out a scheme for the use of such video films as are available from different sources. This scheme should be integrated with the teaching schedule. Video sessions can form the basis for a large variety of classroom practices. Video films may form part of tutorial sessions so that language work can follow from the material presented on the material. Video films may precede group work. The group work can take care of Video-material for language practice of all types. Small scale workshops can proceed from Video material and these can take the form of materials preparation workshops. All the audio-visual devices mentioned above have the hardware and the software components. The teacher's work is to locate, or to do in the class for language or content teaching.

5. Low-cost Instructional Aids for the Classroom

Most teachers shirk away from the use of teaching aids chiefly because teaching aids have unique problems of their own such as : 1. the preparation of aids or their procurement including their cost, 2. preserving these aids including cumbersome maintenance, and 3. procuring these for specific classroom purposes. There are factors beyond the ability of the teachers such as the cost and the facility for preservation of aides, but for the creative and resourceful teacher these pose no problems because the present day concept of *low-cost instructional aids* has come as a boon to the teacher of English and other subjects to meet several such problems. Technological aids are expensive, the maintenance difficulty and the use relativity cumbersome. The school should have a full-time technician or a teacher trained in educational technology and paid for the technical work. All subjects will be able to use his services according to a regular schedule that takes care of areas in particular subjects that can be dealt with better using a technological aid. The teacher should have the know-how of 1. the unit of material where an aid is necessary, 2. the step of teaching where it becomes most effective and relevant, 3. the synthesis that he can achieve between the teaching unit and the aid, 4. the classroom interaction that the aid can help generate, and 5. the follow-up work that may become necessary to ensure optimum benefit in the use of a particular aid. The following low-cost aids can be prepared by the teacher on his own initiative with considerably less cost that any school can afford:

1. *Drawings*: Drawings should not bring to our minds those beautiful sketched panoramic scenes or life-like and life-size paintings

that only affluent artists are capable of. Drawings can be sketchy, simple, uni-coloured and mounted on simple, cheap cardboards or unmounted for the sake of preserving. The teacher of English or other subjects before the school year begins should prepare an inventory of areas where drawings of several kinds can be of use. This can be done as a team. These areas are closely linked to the syllabus and the courses. The scheme should have a coverage for the whole year. Right at the start of the year the topics for the drawings should be distributed to students at higher classes, especially those who have a knack to draw. Together with the work of the students, the teacher can make arrangements to obtain a sizeable number of pictures to draw. Right from the start of the school year the teachers of English and other languages like Hindi can begin using these drawings as they are collected. In one year a comprehensive set can be prepared, labelled, numbered and kept in safety so that the following year onwards these are at the disposal of the class and the teacher to be used as part of regular teaching. The drawings can be prepared specifically geared to the needs of teaching language materials or content units.

2. *Commercial Pictures*: Another low-cost instructional aid are the commercial pictures available in the market. These pictures are available from almost all bookstalls and cover a variety of aspects to be dealt with in the classroom. Such pictures are relatively cheap and all schools can afford to secure these. The problem lies not the procurement of these pictures but in maintenance and the use of them. Unless they constitute part of an overall scheme as mentioned above in the case of the drawings, there is absolutely no use of filling the school libraries or reading rooms with bulks of these pictures. The teachers of English and other subjects should have a scheme, which tells them (a) what pictures are available in the school, (b) where to locate these without too much labour, (c) as part of which unit a particular picture should be used, and (d) how effectively the picture can form part of a technique.

3. *Picture Cards*: Commercially available pictures may not always suit to the very specific use for which the teacher requires a set of pictures. The teacher will need small and single pictures which he may use for practice in general or for group work. These pictures can be mounted on cards and the set can be used by the teacher for a variety of pictorial illustrative purposes, and as picture aids. Picture cards should be relatively small in size so that these cards can easily be distributed to

the class unlike big, commercially available pictures, and preserved easily for further use. Picture cards are of specific use when we provide communicative activities to the class in the teaching of grammar and vocabulary. Using the pictures the students can undertake interquestioning and do language work orally or in writing. Even the preparation and use of these picture cards should not be a haphazard affair, instead the whole thing should schematised and should constitute part of an overall plan in teaching the units for the term or the year.

4. *Flash Cards*: In all the cases above the content-matter is a picture or a drawing depicting a thing or a situation which the student will use as the basis for language recognition or production. There can be instructional aids like the flashcards which need not contain pictures or drawings of any kind but pure language material. We shall distinguish picture cards from flash cards in this specific sense although in several instances teachers identify these two. Flash cards are small cards, again, big enough to carry on it: 1. parts of sentences, 2. phrases, 3. single words, 4. minimal pairs and so on. Flash cards are useful for the teaching of grammar and vocabulary especially at the meaningful/communicative step. If carefully used flash cards can form material for the Drill part of the lesson, to present patterns for the drill. The teacher can prepare flash cards easily and store them easily in well-grouped packs. These should easily be retrievable when the occasion arises for their use in line with the syllabus or course material. Subjects like geography can use flash cards or picture cards when the consolidation or review work is done. The recognition element involved in the use of the flash cards can be tapped for the teaching of content-specific lessons.

5. *Flashboard*: All flash cards need not be larger than a specific size. Flash cards can be displayed casually and easily by the teacher or by he students in group work. A flash board is conceived of as an aid larger in size but unlike a chart a flashboard can be manipulated for a variety of purposes. Unlike a picture chart the flashboard contains only language material. This language material can be organised and reorganised on the flash board itself to produce new phrases, sentences and patterns. Unlike the flash cards the flash board cannot be placed in the hands of students. The teacher has to put it up before the class for the students to produce new patterns of language guided by the teacher. A flash board should be made out of a cardboard with facility to mount other pieces on it to arrange patterns of English. In the teaching of

pronunciation, for instance, words with the same pronunciation can be arranged on the board by the students against a list of words that is stable on the board. Minimal pairs can be arranged similarly in the teaching of pronunciation. In this manner flashboards serve a very useful purpose.

6. *Charts*: Charts are commercially available material with a variety of pictures on them or drawn on a large-scale for specific purposes. Instead of letting publishers of charts to do the work in a haphazard manner, schools in particular regions should workout topics and areas on which charts can be produced. English language charts have great scope in this regard. Registers, themes and topics should be based on graded and organised language material: structures and vocabulary so that these charts have full curricular relevance. Once such sets are available schools should be able to buy these and put them at the disposal of teachers of English. As mentioned in the case of pictures and drawings these charts should be integrated into the teaching scheme so that the teacher knows where to look for a chart when he is in need of one. Charts are of special help in the teaching of oral compositions and picture (oral) compositions. An oral composition will use a picture/chart only at the Initial Work, but the actual development of the material for the composition will be based only on a picture or chart and not on the learner's imagination as in a pure oral composition. Charts with language material especially dialogues can help teaching conversational English. Charts with register-based words can help teach vocabulary.

7. *Flannel Board*: A flannel board is a unique kind of instructional aid in the sense that it becomes most attractive if properly used. A flannel board can be made out of a wooden or cardboard base covered with flannel cloth. It is commercially available in several attractive colours. These boards can have language material or pictures printed or written on flannel pieces and stuck to it. These flannel pieces can be taken out easily and re-stuck depending on the particular need. These are very attractive instructional aids that can be prepared at very low cost. Flannel boards are useful for both language-specific and content-specific teaching situations. A science classroom can have a flannel board used for illustrating a large variety of plant, animal and natural functions. An English classroom has greatest scope for the use of the flannel board. In the teaching of spoken English a flannel board can

help the presentation and organisation of words belonging to various stress groups, pronunciation groups etc. The teaching of grammar can use the flannel board for drill, and communicative practice. Similarly all the lessons in English have scope for the use of the flannel board and make the lesson interesting and attractive to students.

8. *Puzzle Cards*: Like picture cards and flash cards we have another variety of teaching aid in the form of puzzle cards. While picture cards have one picture on a card, flash cards have some unit of language on a card, puzzle cards can present to the class a variety of language games. Language games as are available in W.R. Lee's *Language Games for English* or William Mackey's: *Language Teaching Analysis* can provide the teacher of English with a variety of games than can be played through puzzle cards. Apart from these, the teacher can work out very simple puzzles for the class using English vocabulary, that can be played by organising puzzle cards. Many kinds of word-building and sentence building games can be played through an imaginative use of the puzzle cards. All language games are adequate for creating communicative contexts for the communicative use of language as part of the communicative activities in the teaching of grammar, vocabulary and a variety of composition.

9. *Models for the Classroom*: The preparation of models of several kinds can be undertaken for the teaching of second languages and other subjects. Models have great scope in the teaching of science subject with reference to the anatomy and physiology of animals and plants as well the natural phenomena with which students will be acquainted. Models are rudimentary replication of 1. buildings, 2. things, 3. situations and 4. plants and animals. These models can prepared by students at higher levels with the guidance of teacher, for the children of lower classes. Thermocol is the best material available these days for the preparation of models since these can be cut, shaped and joined as we wish. Apart from this one can make use of wood, cardboard, flannel, cotton, coarse cloth etc., for the preparation of low-cost but very useful teaching aids in the form of models. These models can be used for a variety of instructional situations. While two-dimensional material like pictures or charts can be preserved conveniently, three dimensional materials are hard to store and take care of for further use. This is a major problem that teachers have to face in the use of models as instructional aids.

10. *Puppets for Classroom*: Puppets and puppetry constitute another area of very useful instructional aids. With some creative imagination and experience teachers can use the instructional potential of puppetry. At the professional level puppetry and ventriloquism are artistic and require considerable training. But an enthusiastic teacher can very well employ this art (puppetry) on a minor scale. A large variety of communicative situations in the teaching of English can be enacted and illustrated to children especially in lower classes using rudimentary types of puppets. A few children in a class may be trained to handle puppets and produce the language. It is not necessary for every one to learn to use puppets in the class. While one or two children exhibit the puppet action other students can produce language as it happens in the case of the technique of miming. In miming one does the action another make a sentences that illustrate the action in detail.

11. *Masks for Personification*: Communicative language teaching has numerous communicative contexts that can be effectively practical using a variety of masks for personification. Masks are easy to prepare, easy to use and easy to preserve. Masks can be made of paper or cloth; the images can be of people or animals. The masks can represent professions and occupations, and the students wearing these masks can create very amusing communicative situations using dialogues. The use of the masks will add to the glamour and realism that such communicative situation can project in the classroom.

12. *Albums*: The class can undertake the preparation of albums for several purposes. Albums can be chiefly picture albums for language teaching and learning purposes. Unlike photographs or stamps picture albums are easy to prepare, keep and use. Children of lower or higher classes will be fascinated to prepare register_based picture albums and use these albums in learning situation. The use of these depend on the creative sense of the teacher with reference to the teaching contexts. All the instructional aids mentioned above are low-cost and have great instructional potential when applied teaching situations.

6. Guide-lines in the Preparation of Low-cost Aids

Instructional aids as we have seen are many and many and varied, and are so relevant to classroom teaching that the language teacher and the subject teacher alike cannot afford to neglect the use of one form of such aid or other. Low-cost aids as envisaged in the present work can be prepared, maintained and used by all teachers at all levels irrespective of their urban of rural background. A few important guide-lines will be hopeful for the teacher of English, second languages and other subjects in their attempt to produce and use low-cost teaching aids:

1. *The Need for a Scheme*: The preparation and use of instructional aids cannot materialise effectively unless guided by a well-worked out scheme. Preparation and use of any aid should not lend itself to randomness. All this would mean planning, cost and energy. Every simple picture prepared by the teacher or the student is a valuable resource that can be recurringly made use of. The teachers of English should join hands and work out a scheme for the whole year or at least for a term in order to prepare instructional aids. First, we should identify the language material on the syllabus and in the textbook that require instructional aids without the help of which teaching the item would be impossible. There will also be a group of language items which can be taught without any such aid, but the use of an aid will make the work far easier. In the first group an aid becomes obligatory while in the second group the teachers have an option to have aids or not.

Once a list of the kind mentioned above is prepared, the schematisation of the use of these aids have to be worked out. The same aid can perhaps be used by different teachers for the teaching of different units. The scheme can have a distribution of topics on the basis of subjects to which the topic will belong.

2. *Allocation of the Kinds of Aids*: Once the list of aids is finalised and its subject-wise distribution is taken care of if found alright, the next step is to see what kind of an aid should be prepared for each item. The teachers‘ own creative imagination will help produce aids that are not included in my list; I do not claim the list of instructional aids to be comprehensive. The teachers concerned will make an allocation of all kinds of instructional aids against the language items or topics that have been listed. One language item or one content-specific topic may require a chart while another will require a model. This allocation of aid is very important since it can save redundancy in the preparation of aids as well as ensure a full coverage of the areas where instructional aids become necessary.

3. The next step in the preparation of low-cost aids is the actual allocation of work to different groups of people. It is not necessary for

the teachers to labour over such aids. The preparation can be undertaken in several ways. The most feasible way is to pass on the list of instructional aids to a college of Education where as part of the course the student teachers undertake the preparation of instructional aids. The school will give the full list or part of it to the college or department which uses this list for the student teachers to prepare instructional aids. This arrangement can produce excellent results since the preparation of the aids will be undertaken by grown-up students with a motivation that the school teacher or the pupils may not have. The only problem that might arise from this arrangement is that the instructional aids as the regular submissions of the students can be at the disposal of the school probably only in the following year.

4. Another way of procuring these aids is to use the services of teachers and students at higher levels who are willing and able to lene a helping hand and take up the responsibility of preparing the aids. For this too the allocation has to be make by the group who has taken up the overall responsibility for the preparation of the aids. In this undertaking we should not look so much for the quality of the aid prepared; whatever is prepared is only an instructional aid and the only criteria should be whether the aid serves the purpose for which it is meant.

5. Instructional aids should be accessible to the teacher as and when he needs it for use in the classroom. The list prepared as part of the scheme can tell him what to look for and where to look for an aid. The teacher can make regular and elaborate use of aids like the charts, picture cards, and flash cards as these have multidimensional function to perform. A set of picture cards can be used for the production of interactional situations during group work not only with reference to any one unit but the set can be found useful in a number of situation. The same picture can be used for teaching grammatical items once, vocabulary on another and an oral composition on a third occasion. In other words, the teacher who makes up his mind to use instructional aids have ample opportunities to yoke these various aids to tasks.

6. Instructional aids are only a means to the basic work in the classroom. The teacher's aim is either language work or work on a unit of content-matter. Especially with reference to language this point is very significant. The instructional aid, or any interactional or communicative situation for that matter should not come on the way to the understanding or practice of the actual language.

In other words these materials or situations should never distract students from paying attention to the language. Often the teacher creates a lot of noise situations in the class and children enjoy everything. Even if enjoyment is a little less, the learning situations, the learning stimuli provided should have a definite direction so that at the end of all the gymnastics some learning should take place. If language teaching can be undertaken in interesting contexts with some degree of fun it is fine; but fun should not be an aim itself. We may have a lot of fun in teaching English through an indiscriminate use of the regional language; but it serves absolutely no purpose. The same is true of the use of instructional aids in the classroom. With a sense of definite direction, an awareness of the concrete needs of the students and of the teachers's purpose on hand, instructional aids can turn classroom teaching into a highly productive experience.

10

THE ACADEMIC SKILL OF REFERENCE

1. Aspects of Academic Skills

The term academic skills has assumed a new dimension with the recent development of *English for Academic Purposes*. English for academic purposes takes care of a large variety of skills and aspects of English language that become essential to achieve proficiency in undertaking higher studies in English. By academic skills in the present context we mean all the component skills that a student, a teacher, or an academic in any field of enquiry require in order to function effectively. Without the development of these skills which include a variety of study skills a student who is in pursuit of academic excellence of any kind will remain stranded.

Academic skills are component skills of a system that we shall call *Academic Performance or Scholarship*. The following are the essential academic skills of Academic Performance : 1. The skill of public speaking, 2. the skill of reading, 3. the skill of reference, 4. the skill of note-taking from talks, 5. the skill of note-taking from reading, 6. the skill of oral expression, 7. the skill of creative writing, 8. the skill of organising academic procedures such as workshops, 9. the skill of preparing a talk, and 10. the skill of academic investigation. Some of these may have overlaps, yet every one of them constitutes a component of what we are able to call Academic Performance, a phenomenon that makes an academic a genius or a pauper.

Academic Performance as a system can be defined, analysed,

investigated into and evaluated. In other words the present work envisages this as a concrete and dynamic system with possibilities of enhancement and perfection as well as degeneration. The components that we have examined are skills. By skills we mean aspects of performance that are basically habits involving further component habits of an elementary kind. These skills are definable, analysable, can be investigated into and can be evaluated on an individual basis. These are aspects that render a system or a sub-system its authenticity and perfection. As academic skills these components that begin from a basis in an individual, develop in the individual through practice and habit formation, function in the individual with reference to academic activities of a variety of kinds, and lastly mature in the individual with greater exposure to very Specific and Specialised involvement.

Academic skills are *techniques* that contribute to the academic development and perfection of the individual. As techniques these skills have a procedural and functional perspective. The academic skill of public speaking, for instance is procedural and functional. Public speaking is an event, a structured system, as well as a phenomenon; but for present purposes we are viewing this phenomenon as a function, as a skill involving analysable components of several kinds that in themselves are component habits. Gesticulation, for instance, is such a component habit as part of the skill of public speaking. The totality of these component habits depending on the degree to which these are taken care of will decide the quality of an individual's public speaking performance as an academic performance. Hence public speaking as an academic skill can be called a global technique of academic performance, and the component skill of gesticulation can be called a technique of public speaking.

Academic skills, again, constitute the creative expression of the human person in coordinating his component abilities, attitudes and aptitudes. The whole phenomenon of academic performance as a system is creative and purposeful highly controlled by the creative bents of the human personality. A resourceful teacher is what he is primarily because of the full exploitation of these creative bents of the human personality. Had all this been merely habit formation on the foundation of the stimulus - response phenomenon, then we would never have witnessed a perfection beyond that of the average professional. Academic skills are capable of leading us to the very heights of perfection precisely because these skills have their foundation on the creative intelligence of the human personality. The habit formation part of it is just a means to the perfection that an individual is capable of attaining in the acquisition and expression of these skills. The academic skills for the attainment of similar perfection in an academic calls for intense attention, training and follow-up so that the individual's full creative resources are exploited for excellence in areas of academic performance.

2. Academic Skills for the Teacher

The teacher in the classroom is attempting to achieve a synthesis of two inter-related systems: 1. classroom teaching as a system, and 2. the teacher's own performance as another system. In the first section we examined the general basis of what the latter system is. Classroom teaching as a system has been our preoccupation in all the foregoing chapters. The teacher's own performance in all the foregoing chapters. The teacher's own performance we now view as Academic Performance whose scope as we seen is very large. By the teacher's performance we mean the academic quality of a number of things that form part of his performance.

1. *The skill of public speaking* that constitutes a major and conspicuous component of the teacher's academic performance. By public speaking we not only mean the ability of rhetories that makes an individual a successful orator on the stage, but also public speaking means *the ability to face an audience*, talk to them using acceptable and formal language, and communicate to them units of information in a most economic and intelligeable manner. The teacher is essentially a public speaker. He not only has to face his class but also other audiences on several occasions. He may not use the techniques of rhetories in an all their perfection, but he has to train himself in the elements or rudiments of public speaking. The following aspects will help him do well in the classroom from the view point of public speaking : 1. proficiency in the language of communication (at least those aspects that will require as a teacher), 2. ability to think in an organised manner while speaking, 3. ability to convey his content matter to the audience with the same organisation, 4. meaningful contact with the audience, 5. a well-developed voice for one's work, 6. ability to keep the full attention of the audience while working, 7. ability to bring in variety in the techniques used in presenting one's material, and 8. ability to

introduce a reasonable degree of interaction with the audience. These components go into the making of effective public speaking as a skill for the teacher in the classroom.

2. *The skill of reading* enables the teacher keep abreast to the latest developments in his field of study. Reading is the backbone of teaching profession and the teacher will find himself totally at loss if he lags behind in reading. As a skill of Academic Performance reading constitutes the basis for the teacher's personal study, for dealing with the background material of his classroom work, for the course material as such, and for whatever professional involvement he has as a teacher.

3. *The skill of reference* is exactly the present concern and the details will be examined in the following sections. Reference skills as these are generally known have a number of aspects, that are intimately linked to the teacher's work in the classroom. Reference Constitutes the ability that the teacher requires to gather material, gather information, work on the texts on hand, refer to source books, reference books, dictionaries etc., collage information, preserve a variety of information that he needs, and retrieve the information and the material as and when he needs to use them. Reference skills are very basic to the making of an effective teacher.

4. *The Skill of Note-taking from Talks* : A well-trained student knows the art of note-taking from talks, lectures and classes. But it mostly happens that people find note-taking a cumbersome activity and a challenging one. Note-taking from talks does not in any way become part of classroom teaching for the teacher. But the teacher needs to be trained in this academic skill. There will arise several occasions when the teacher will attend seminars and inservice courses, or talks given by guest speakers in a neighbouring university which he will be asked to attend. Again for the teacher may have to go for studies as part of his up-gradation programme. In all such instances note-taking plays a central role in the teacher's career. This skill involves components such as : 1. Well-trained listening to the grasp the content matter, 2. a recorganisation of the material in one's mind as the talk goes on, 3. a schematisation of the material to do meaningful recording, 4. organising the material on a continuous basis as the talk goes on, 5. simultaneous listening and recording (writing) ability, 6. the ability to sift from the talk the central points and leave out details, 7. to keep in mind the overall content of the talk while jotting down the material,

and 8. the ability to work out further details later establishing a link between the content listened to and the material recorded on paper.

5. *The Skill of Note-taking from Reading*. Note-taking from reading constitutes another important and definable academic skill that is a component of Academic Performance. Note-taking from reading is relatively easier than note-taking from talks. It is called a skill because it is a sub-system itself having components and requires attention and training to function well. More than the skill related to talks the teacher either in school and more so in collages and universities need to develop this skill because of the great relevance reading has to the profession of teaching. The details of note-taking from reading will be examined in one of the following sections.

6. *The Skill of Oral Expression* : The skill of public speaking and oral expression overlap to some extent. By oral expression we mean the teacher's ability to *develop an oral discourse* using the second language in particular. Here the aspects of rhetorics stressed in public speaking are not so much emphasised. Oral expression is an academic skill that enables the teacher in the class or on other formal occasions to construct a discourse in the form of narration or a talk. The most important component is the ability to have organised thinking through the second language and an organised and logical presentation of the material with reasonable fluency.

7. *The Skill of Creative Writing*: Written expression is the ability to construct a discourse in writing. Writing is a basic language skill. With reference to the teacher this skill of writing assumes a new dimension. The teacher should not only know how to do ordinary writing in good language but also develop the ability to make original and creative writing of at least elementary kind. This skill should find development from one's student days by attempting to write essays and material with a touch of originality. The teacher should build on this training and should develop the art of creative writing.

8. *The Skill of Organising Academic Activities*: The present work at large is concerned about the creative application of academic procedures of all kinds to the classroom. As such the teacher should possess the academic skill of creative organisation of academic activities to provide students with a greater range of satisfying learning experiences. This skill can be developed by greater exposure into co-

curricular activities and by a conscious effort to develop the organisational skill. The skill involves all component abilities right from the planning stage upto the evaluation of the work to judge the effectiveness of the work undertaken.

9. *The Skill of Preparing a Talk* : By talk we mean any narrative or expository activity that the teacher might undertake from time to time both in the class as well as outside. Any talk would involve preparation of some kind so that the teacher would have the necessary confidence at the time of the work. There are several ways of preparing a talk depending on the seriousness involved. This would mean the use of the reference skills that we shall be looking into in detail, gathering points necessary for the talk, organising the points with a definite direction, and developing a habit of linking the prepared material and the actual talk. Preparing a lecture or a talk of any kind thus involves a definable set of component skills that require independent analysis.

10. *The Skill of Academic Investigation* : Academic investigation or enquiry or research, a process known under a variety of names, is an academic skill of high standing. Right from the preparation of a talk or a paper upto a full-fledged work like a Ph.D. thesis what is inherently involved is an academic skill that we call academic investigation or research. Research is a very complex skill that involves a large number of component habits including many of those we have already seen. But at the core of it all we have a very sensitive and definable skill, the skill of investigation. It consists in a search for 1. information, 2. data where necessary, 3. materials that will go into the writing, 4. documents for authenticity, and 5. people where first hand information becomes necessary. A simple project that a student undertakes in school or an action research a teacher can undertake with reference to his own teaching problems with all involve the skill of academic investigation.

The skill mentioned above are all academic skills that constitute part of what we have called Academic Performance. At the component level these seem to be far too elementary and prime notions to deal with seriously. But this is not so. Every one of the component habits that go into the making of an academic skill is definable and analysable and hence has a role to play in the development of the specific skill. These skills together will go into the making of what we call a resourceful teacher.

3. Aspects of Reference Skills

Reference skills constitute an area which the teacher cannot afford to neglect as this has got much to do with the quality work he is expected to do in the classroom. Reference skills or what I have referred to earlier as the skill of reference skills or what I have referred to earlier as the skill of reference includes all those activities that the teacher has to undertake to acquire information a variety of sources in order to help his teaching work as a whole. The teacher is expected to know how to refer to materials to *clarify information* related to the instructional material he has to teach in the class. He has to move out of the narrow bounds of the text-book on the one hand and know in depth what the instructional materials actually mean. These are going to be lexical items whose meaning he does not know, names whose background is not part of his knowledge, information which he cannot explain to the class, authors about whom he has no information, the time (year) in which certain relevant events took place, the sequence of certain historical events, and the list can go on where the teacher has to go out of the bounds of the textbook to clarify and provide information to the class. All this means scientific reference work on his part for which the skills needs to be developed.

The teacher should know how to refer to materials, again, to *broaden his information.* Clarification of things forming part of the course is most fundamental and unavoidable. Similarly, a resourceful teacher cannot be contented with the skeletal knowledge he has on the subject which just enables him to teach the minimum things in the class, or just to explain a lesson in the class. The resourceful teacher will be contented only with a much broader knowledge that will help him do quality work in the class. Reference skill is his aid to achieve this, refers to books immediately related to the lessons of the text, books that will bring him interesting aspects of related information that the class will enjoy, magazines and periodicals which will bring him current and relevant information what goes on around the world, and what goes on particularly in his field of study.

Reference Skills become important for the teacher of English because these skills are part of the *students' training*. The use of dictionaries, the use of encyclopaedias, the use of Year Books, locating and using a library book from the small school library, and using relevant information from magazines and periodicals for his own follow-up studies and so on. All these involve reference skills for which the class should be given some degree of training. The teacher thus need to develop the skill of reference in its variety of components to help students know some essentials of reference work and use this knowledge for his academic pursuit.

What exactly are these reference skills ? 1. The use of a dictionary with a level of efficiency; 2. the use of source-books and manuals; 3. the use of encyclopaedias and Year Books; 4. the use of documents for research; 5. general reference for purposes of study; 6. ability to look for lists of books, 7. the skill of using the library catalogue, 8. the skill of locating books in a library, 9. ability to locate exact information, 10. ability to sift relevant material from source books, 11. the skill of taking notes from source and reference books, 12. the skill of organising the information for later use, 13. the skill of collating materials gathers from different sources(preservation), and 14. the skill of retrieving information / materials for specific writing.

Reference skills thus consists of a large number of components as mentioned above which call for the exercise of one's mind, practice and intelligent manipulation of the resources around.

The teacher cannot rise above a level of academic performance unless he masters the science of using information and materials available around him for a specific academic purposes. There can be inservice courses of a variety of kinds for the teacher of English in particular and second languages in general to be well-informed about and trained in all aspects of academic skills in general and reference skills in particular. It is not possible to educate students in all the components of reference skills mentioned above unless particular orientation courses and workshops are arranged for them in school. Teachers on the other hand should not only know these perspectives in their details but more important they should try to obtain practice in the optimum use of reference skills for study purposes.

4. The Skill of Using Dictionaries

A dictionary is a compendium of words that are part of a language. In linguistics the word *lexicon* indicates the total list of the lexical items that constitutes part of the language. A lexical item is the technical term for a word. The dictionary is a constant companion for every educated person: the student, the teacher and the professional require the dictionary for constant reference. What do we get-out of a dictionary ? The teacher who is dictionary: 1. Word reference, 2. connotations and extensions of words, 3. levels of meanings and lexical homonymy, 4. word-ethymology that will be required for greater understanding of the meaning, 5. regional varieties to which English words belong and the regional specifications (e.g. American Vs British English), 6. pronunciation of words, 7. stress pattern of words, 8. exact usage for which the dictionary provides help, 9. cross-reference between synonymous and homophonous words, and 10. vocabulary enrichment for which the dictionary is of great use. An awareness of these intimate aspects of a dictionary helps the teacher make greater use of it in his attempts to become a better teacher of English, for instance.

1. *Word reference* is basic to the use of a dictionary. The teacher will be required to take up a dictionary for reference primarily when he comes across a new word or expression in his teaching material, general reading or in a talk that he listened to. He looks up in the dictionary in these particular cases for the regular and first meaning of a lexical item. The word is totally unknown to him or the exact meaning of the word in that communicative context is not grasped by him. The dictionary comes handy for him to find out these aspects. Out of a number of options provided in the dictionary he will choose a meaning that he feels is contextually correct.

2. *Connotations and extensions* (denotations) of words constitute another aspect that the teacher can look for in dictionaries. Connotation means the semantic depth of a word i.e. the number of units of meaning that go into the structure of a word. The word 'father' in English has deeper connotations or levels of meaning in English than its counterpart in Indian languages. The term 'uncle' has deeper connotations in English than its counterparts in Indian languages. While 'uncle' indicates more than one relationship, Indian languages have a specific word for every relationship that the word 'uncle' indicates in English. By extension or denotation we mean the number of subgroups, individuals or categories covered by the lexical item. In English 'sister' includes a wider category of individuals than its counterpart in Indian languages. The word 'breakfast' has a distribution of cases of eating narrower than any similar word such as 'nasta' in Hindi. The dictionary comes to the teacher's

help in finding out the depth and extension of the meaning of a lexical item.

3. *Levels of meanings* that the dictionary provides come to the teacher's help as part of his reference. By levels I mean something different from what we have seen above. These are the *different meanings* of a specific word indicated in the dictionary. This includes *lexical homonymy*. The words bark, spring, date, bank, host etc. mean very different and totally unrelated things under one and the same phonological and orthographic form. These are a few examples of hundreds of such lexical items in English which the dictionary helps the teacher to identify with reference to a context in which the item occurs.

4. *Lexical etymology*: The teacher can acquaint himself with the etymology of words at different levels in different dictionaries. The dictionary tells him whether a word has a Latin, Greek, French, Arabic, Indian or African origin. We have English words that have their etymological roots in all these languages apart from the Anglo-Saxon and Scandinavian stocks of lexical items. The Latin and Greek stems of English words tell us in depth what the word should exactly mean, apart from the indication the entry in the dictionary gives about the current meaning. The teacher's understanding of the etymological rudiments will help him function better in the classroom as a teacher of English.

5. *Regional Varieties*: Every English dictionary today gives indication as to whether a word specifically belongs to American or British English or part of the variety of English used in Australia, Canada or other countries where English is used as the native language. There are dictionaries of American English which makes special mention only of words of British, Canadian or Australian origin and vice-versa. The dictionary makes special mention of American English Pronunciation if the dictionary is of British English. The teacher should make a special study of the distinction between regional varieties of English especially of those words that occur in our day-to-day use such as : direction, dimension, advertisement, civilisation, office and secretary. The dictionary also indicates words that are used commonly only in a given regional variety such as 'guy, gas (perol), corn (maze)' used in American English.

6. *Pronunciation and Spellings*: The dictionary is at the teacher's disposal to ensure the correct pronunciation of the English words on the one hand and spellings on the other. The pronunciation is indicated through general *orthographic code* or in *phonetic notation*. In either ways the teacher will be able to look into the exact pronunciation and spelling system. Both the codes can be picked up easily by the teacher with a little experience.

The dictionary comes to the teacher's help not only in these areas. Every English word has a *specific stress*. The teacher should develop a consciousness of this *stress specifications* of English words, look up in the dictionary for the *stress assignment*, both primary and secondary in the case of polysyllabic words, and attempt to speak English in the class using the correct pronunciation and stress. Some dictionaries not only indicate the meanings, pronunciation and the orthographic specifications but also the *most typical usage* of a lexical item. The dictionary also indicates where there is *grammatical homonymy* i.e. different uses of the same grammatical item, especially as different categories, e.g. 'over'. The dictionary helps also develop *cross-reference* between words and find out several synonymous forms of the same word with a degree of fluctuations in meaning elements. Lastly the teacher can use the dictionary for *vocabulary enrichment.* He is not expected to commit lexical items to memory; at leisure hours looking up through the dictionary will bring back to memory words that we have learned and these become part of our word stock. A dictionary is a teacher's constant companion and the habit of dictionary reference should be passed on to one's class as part of our regular classroom teaching.

5. The Use of Encyclopaedias and Year Books

The dictionary is the most basic reference material that the teacher should have on hand for ready use. Another important *Source of information* is the encyclopaedia. While the dictionary is a compendium of lexical items that constitute part of the total list of words in the language, an encyclopaedia is a *compendium of information* which we can turn to when we are short of some information of a well-defined kind. The information that the encyclopaedia gives us can be called *classified information* which we require for undertaking a large variety of academic activities including teaching, writing and journalism.

The encyclopaedia is a ready reference material for any one who undertakes the following academic activities: 1. Contribution to journalism, 2. Contribution articles and features to professional and popular magazines and periodicals, 3. undertaking projects of comprehensive coverage on historical places and historical persons, 4. undertaking projects on persons or organisations which have made significant contributions to the cause of humanity at large, and 5. undertaking writing to books in any area of specialisation. Encyclopaedias are the rich source books which authors and scholars turn to for any kind of classified information.

The teacher of English as well as other subjects have reasons to turn to this great compendium of knowledge.

A large variety of valuable Encyclopedias is available today in the Market. The teacher can use the encyclopedia for a variety of purposes other than those mentioned above that are of a scholarly nature. The following are the uses he can have of the compendium:

(a) Encyclopedias contain *scientific definitions* of technical, scientific, medical and technological vocabulary that the teacher may have to refer to from time to time especially if he undertakes any work of a scholarly or scientific nature. Definitions that encyclopaedias offer will be most comprehensive and will contain information from different perspectives.

(b) Encyclopaedias contain component analysis of all conceivable systems that scholars have been able to classify for purposes of research and study. Any system that constitutes part of any discipline in particular, or systems that are part of general nature are classified in encyclopaedias with detailed reference to their components. 'United Nations' as a system will be divided and analysed into its component and member organisations and bodies in regard to their structure and specific functions.

(c) The teacher finds facts about *historical events* that are otherwise not accessible easily as fully classified information except in technical book on History. Since encyclopaedias are schematised in alphabetical order, it is far easier to locate such information in an encyclopaedia than in books on History.

(d) The teacher can find facts about *historical personalities* of great standing, about whom only encyclopaedias speak authoritatively and in considerable detail. Such details that can be easily obtainable from a handy number of an encyclopaedia would otherwise take considerable time and energy to locate from other source books. While teaching a lesson in the textbook the teacher may need information regarding historical persons that figure in the lesson. He then needs only to turn to the encyclopaedia.

(e) The teacher can find facts about *places of historical*, cultural and political importance which often form part of his teaching. Going about groping in the dark for information about such places would prove futile. The encyclopaedia is the answer to this relevant need of the teacher.

(f) No teacher can know or need to know everything about all disciplines and *fields of studies*. On numerous occasions the teacher is required to know facts, theories, or details of a superfluous kind for his personal study or classroom teaching. General information about all disciplines is available in encyclopaedias and the teacher will such details enough for his practical purpose to fill in gaps in his own knowledge. Latest editions of encyclopaedias provide a reasonably big coverage of all important fields of study that can come under classified information.

Similarly, the teacher will find the Year Book useful in locating detailed information about National life, data about historical events in Indian and in the World and geographical as well as astronomical facts. The Year Book is a compendium chiefly bringing to the readers all facts, figures and classified information that are particularly *relevant to the current year,* as well as general facts, figures and *information of a general type*. For the teacher to have the relevant details of the Asian Games or 1984 Olympics, the encyclopedia will not be any help soon after the events have finished, but the Year Book can provide all the necessary information. The Year Book can again, provide information about current and past sports events, political events, political leaders, Nobel Prize Winners and Winners of all International Awards. The Year Book like the encyclopaedia is a compendium, but the encyclopaedia provides classified information of permanent nature with special reference to the past; the Year Book on the other hand gives all information about major events upto the current year. Both these Source books are most handy to the teacher to improve his scholarship.

6. General Reference for Study Purposes

Reference skills include not only making proper use of dictionaries and encyclopaedias but also the ability to use general reference books from a library for personal study or research. Every teacher depends upon considerable degree of reading to keep himself abreast to the latest knowledge available in books and magazines. If not every teacher needs to read a few books to obtain the *background information* on which the lessons in the textbook are based. The teacher may have to present a paper at a seminar, participate in a materials preparation worship, contribute a short paper to the school magazine or to any outside, organise an action research, give a talk on his own subject of specialisation to other teachers in the school and a number of involvements of this kind can be envisaged whether library reference will be required. The following details may be kept in mind in this regard.

1. *The use of bibliography*: In order to find out a few books that will help the teacher gather material for the preparation of a short paper on 'Co-curricular Activitres', he attempts to have access to a bibliography or reading list. A bibliography may be available from a book on the subject that he has on hand, another seminar paper or article that the teacher has located on a logic in the same area of study, a resource person who will be able to provide a list of reference books, or as the last resort, the teacher will go to an Education Library and look through the *library catalogue* on for a few books on the subject of his requirement. The library catalogue presents in alphabetical order the information in two ways: 1. Authorwise and 2. Subjectwise. Looking through the subjectwise index the teacher can locate books on the subject if available in the library.

2. *Locating a reference book*: The teacher normally has enough experience in the general use of a library. Still locating a reference book in a library is always a cumbersome work, especially if the library is not well-kept. The catalogue is the source for the full information he requires for this purpose. Either the author index or the title index can provide the *accession number* to the book. We should go straight to the subject section, locate the sub-section in which the book may be found, and look carefully for the accession number on racks. If the book is at

the proper place we easily get Libraries which use a *number system* for subject sections too, the number sequence should guide to the exact spot. The numbers that refer to particular fields of studies will be available at the place where the catalogue is kept. All this is guided by one or other methods of the *International Library Cataloguing System.*

3. *How to locate the relevant information*: Once the book on hand the problem is not solved. For many, locating the exact information or to put it plainly, *using a reference book* is the crux of the problem. The teacher has many techniques at his disposal for the purpose. (a) He looks for reference books after having prepared a framework of the paper he needs to prepare with a few details like sub-topics. This he does himself or with the help of some well-informed person. Once the book is on hand, the teacher looks up in the *content* and *index* sections to see if the topics that he requires are covered in the book. If so, his problem is partly solved. (b) The teacher in the absence of a framework or sub-topics, will sit at his desk quietly and examines the content, index as well the chapters in detail to see if the book provides any material related to his topic. If any is found, he should first jot down on paper the sub-topic and reference page for him to come back on it later. (c) The last resort for the teacher is to read through or skim through the whole book to find out if any relevant material is available in it. This is the last thing to do.

4. *How to Arrive at a Framework and Organisation*: This is another crucial stage that requires training and care, a stage where most people fail. This is an important component of the skill of reference. There are several ways of taking notes from books. Just as mentioned above the teacher either begins with a proforma or framework of the sub-topics and points, or he gradually develops one. If he begins with a framework then we have one method, and if not we have another. In case the teacher has a framework, he looks through the book or reads the book in detail depending on his habit, and looks for sections in the book most relevant to his subject. May be that he located these sections earlier as mentioned above. He then works on that particular section in detail. If he *does not begin with* a framework of sub-topics and points, what he should do first is to pool together sub-topics available from one book after another, sit with the list and *arrive at an organisation*, and leave out sub-topics that he does not include on the list. This would mean that he can conveniently leave out those sections in the

book which are not necessary for his purpose and thereby avoid useless writing.

5. *How to do the exact note-taking from books*: Note-taking from reference books is a systemic activity. The teacher can do it in ways more than one. Once the exact sections are decided upon, he begins the writing work. The best way to do the work is to through points. The teacher reads the material closely, and mentally organises each paragraph, part of a paragraph, or sentences into points using only *phrases*. If a phrase cannot contain all the central information that he requires, he uses full sentences to take down the content-matter. If by training any one cannot convert the material in the book into points, or if he will find it difficult to retrieve the full information from these points with reference to the details in the book, only then should the teacher think of writing down everything that a section in the book gives. Even if this is the method the teacher uses, one should not copy down things word-by-word as this may in turn be carried over to his final work. The teacher will 'translate' the content-matter into his own simple English and thus retain all the information that the book gives.

One by one the teacher will use all the books that he can lay hands on; then begins his actual and final work on the paper that is his target. General reference is not at all easy because our students are never given training in reference skills. Large scale copying is what they usual do in the case of library books. A course on academic skills, reference skills, or study habits should take care of these aspects of academic work and equip our students with the fundamental skills of research that become one way or other necessary in one's later, professional life. Apart from what is mentioned above the teacher should develop a regular *cataloguing*, *filing* and *retrieval system* so that important information can be stored as they come in as part of his reading, contacts, and exposure to the media, and retrieve relevant information for teaching or writing purposes.

Bibliography

Adams, A. New Directions in English Teaching. Falmer Press, London, 1982.

Adair, J. Action-centred Leadership, McGraw-Hill, New York, 1973

Allece, D.W. and K .A.Ryan, Microteaching. Addison - Wesley, Lor.don, 1969

Allen, J.P.B. & S. Pit Carden, Edinburgh Course in Applied Linguistics, OUP London, 1975.

Allen, Harold B. Teaching English as a second language, McGraw-Hill, New York, 1965

Anderson, J.B.H. Durston and C. Katz, Study Methods: A Practical Guide, McGraw-Hill, New York, 1969

Aushel, D.P. The Psychology of Meaningful Verbal Learning, Greece, New York, 1963.

Ayer, A.J. The Problem of Knowledge. London: Macmillan, 1958

Ayer, A.J. Language, Truth and Logic. London: Macmillan, 1966

Barrington, K & I. Rogers, Group Work in Secondary Schools, OUP, 1968

Baruah, T.C. The English Teacher's Handbook. Sterling Publishers, New Delhi, 1984

Berman, Louise 14. New Priorities in the Curriculum , Merrill Publishers, Ohio.

Berlyne, D.E. Conflict, Aransal and Curiosity. McGraw - Hill, New York, 1962

Bowers, Roger Project Planning and Performance. ELT Documents, Oxford, 1980.

Boothman , D.B. etal, Topical Research Workbooks. Longman, 1969.

British Council, Project in Materials Design. ELT Documents, 1980.

British Council Audio-visual materials for English Teaching. London.

Brown, George, Microteaching. A programme of teaching skills. Matheun, London, 1975.

Brumfit, C.J. Language Teachig Projects of the Third World, Oxford, 1980.

Burton, S.H. Mastering English Language. Macmilla.:, 1983.

Bushel, G & F. Morel, English Improvisation Workshop, Evens, London, 1980

Byrne, D., Progressive Picture Composition, Longman, 1966

Byrne, D. & S. Rixon Communication Games, NEFR, ELT guides, 1979

Byrne, D.A. First Book of Board Games. Modern English, London 1980

Byrne, J & Waugh A. Z. g-Zag: An Activity course for children. Oxford, 1979

Candlin, C.N. Communicative Teaching of English, Longman, 1981

Carrier, 14. Topics for Discussion and Language Practice, Hilton, London, 1980

Corden, S.P. English Language Teaching and Television Longman, 1960.

Cartwrigth & Cartwright. Developing Observation Skills, McGraw-Hill, 1974

Cook, M. Interpersonal Perception. Penguin, London, 1970

Carrol, John B., Language and Thought. Prentice Hall, New York, 1964

Cake, George N., From Controlled to Free Composition. ELT, London, 1972

Dale, E. Audio-visual Methods in Teaching, Holt, New York.

Dale, Philip. Language Development structure and function. Dydee Press, Illionois, 1973

Das, Bikram. English for a Developing Country. CIEFL Bulltein 9, 1973

Davis, I.F. The Management of Learning. McGraw-Hill, New York, 1973

Dobinson, H.M. Basic Skills You Need. Nelson, London,1979

Dodson, C.J. Language Teaching and Bilingual Method. Pitman and Sons, 1954

Dunkel, Harold, Second Language Learning
Gum & Co., Boston, 1948

Dunkin, 14 & B. Biddle. The study of Teaching Holt, New York, 1973

Evans, T. Teaching English. Croom Helm, London, 1982

Filipovic, Rudolf (ed.). Active Methods and Modern Aids in Teaching Foreign Language, OHP, London, 1972

Finnochiaro, Mary, Teaching children Foreign Language, McGraw-Hill, New york, 1964.

Fisher and Terry. Children's Languages and the Language Arts. McGraw-Hill, New York, 1977.

Forrester, Jean. Teaching Without Lecturing. OUP, London, 1968

Forrested, Jean. Teaching English to large classes, OUP, London.

Forrested, Jean, Group Work in Colleges, OUP, London.

Foster, B. Changing English Language. Macmillan, London, 1968

Gale, J.A. Group Work in Schools. McGraw - Hills, Australia, 1974

Gartner, Alan, Children Teach Children. Harper, New York, 1941

Gaunlte J.O. Teaching English as a Foreign Language, Macmillan, London, 1957

Gracia, Alfrod De etal. Programmes, Teachers and Machines. MIT Press, Cambridge, 1964

Granger, C. Play Games with English Book. Heinemann, London, 1980.

Grecyberry, J.H. Language, Culture and communication. Sanford Univ. Press, 1975

Gupta, Arun K. Teacher Education, Sterling Publishers, New Delhi, 1984

Gurry, P. Teaching English and Foreign Language, Macmillan,
London, 1962

Hall, Edmand T. The Silent Language. Doubleday & Co., New York, 1959

Hall, Robert A. New Ways to Learn in Foreign Language, Bantam Books, New York, 1960

Harley, B.A. Synthesis of Teaching Methods, McGraw - Hill, Australia.

Harmer, J. The Practice of English Language Teaching. Longman, 1983

Hays, Ann. Planning a Project. ELT Documents, Oxford, 1983.

Heater, J.B. Practice Through Pictures. Longman, London, 1971

Hughes, John B. Longuistics and Language Teaching Random House, New York, 1968

Hymes, Dell H. On Communicative Competence. In Communicative Approach to Language Teaching, by C.J.Brumtit.Oxford, 1966.

Johnson, K& Morrow K. Approaches: A Language Activation Course, Oxford, 1979

Johnson, K. & Morrow K. Communication in the Classroom, Longman, 1981

Jolly, D & P. Early Group Work in ELT. London, British Council.

Jones, L. Graded English Puzzles. Collins, London, 1980

Jordan, R.R. Looking for Information: A Practice Book in reading skills. Longman, 1980

Kay C. & Simmounds FE, English Through Pictures Collins, London, 1980.

Kenneth, Richmond. The concept of Educational Technology. London.

Kopl, Herbert R. The Open Classroom: A Practical Guide to a new Way of Teaching. Viltage Books, New York, 1970.

Koumin, J., Discipline and Group Work Management in Classrooms, Holt, New York, 1970.

Lado, Robert, Language Teaching: A scientific approach, McGraw-Hill, New York, 1964

Layton, David. University Teaching in Transition, New York.

Lee, WIR. Language teaching games and coutesh. Oxford Univ. Press, London.

Leech and Svartvick. A Communicative grammar of English. Longman, 1973.

Left, W.R. The creative Artist at Work. McGraw - Hill, New York, 1974

Little wood, W. Communicative Language Teaching, An Introduction, Cambridge Univ Press, 1983.

Logan & Logan. Design for creative teaching. McGraw-Hill, 1971

Longhton B. Groupwork in Vorwerts - Vorwerts London, British Council.

Lumsdaine, A.A. Teaching Machines and Programmes Learning. N.E.A. Washington, 1960.

Maley, A. Drama Techniques in Language Learning. Cambridge, 1982.

Mathieu. G. Advances in Teaching of Modern Languages. Pergaman, New York, 1966.

Methold, K. Puzzles for English Practice. Longman, 1978

Meyer, M. Sugg. R. Action English. Evans, London, 1979

Mortinen, G. Dramatic Monolognes for listening Comprehension, Cambridge, 1980.

Morrow, K. & Johnson K. Approaches to Lanauges Activities Course, OUP, 1979.

Mukalel, Joseph & Shabbir Ahmed, Teaching English in India. Arya Books, New Delhi, 1984

Mugglestone, Planning and Using Blackboard in Practical Language Teaching. Allen & Unwin, London, 1980.

Munby, J. Read and Twink Longman, London, 1968

Nikson, Marilyn, Educational Technology, London, 1971

Pit Corder, S. English Language Teaching and Television Language, 1965

Politzer, Robert L. Foreign Language Learning: A Linguistic Introduction. Prentice-Hall, 1965

Rivas, Wilga Communicating Naturally in Second Language. Cambridge, 1983

Rivas, Wilga. Teaching Foreign Language Skills. Chicago. 1968

Richy, Robert W. Planning Teaching: An Introduction to Education. McGraw Hill, New York, 1973.

Robinson, W.R. Language and Social Behaviour. Penguin. Middlesex. 1972.

Unesco Press. Word Guide to Higher Education, UNESCO. New York. 1982.

Walls, J. Introduction to Mixed Ability Learning. British Council, London.

Wallace, W.J. Study skills in English. Cambridge Univ. Press, London, 1980.

West, Michael, Trading English in Difficult Circumstances. Language, 1962.

Wheeler, D.K. Curriculum Process, Univ. of London Press.

Widdowson, A.G. Trading Language as Communication. Oxford, 1978.

Wilkins, D.A. Linguistic and Language Teaching. Edward Arnold, London, 1972.

Wrag, E.G. Teaching Teaching. David of Charter, London, 1975.

Wright, A. Games for language Learning, Cambridge Univ. Press, London, 1980.

Index